John Stephen

Bishop Colenso on the Pentateuch:

Quoted and examined; to which are added notes on Part I and strictures on Part II of The Pentateuch and book of Joshua

John Stephen

Bishop Colenso on the Pentateuch:
Quoted and examined; to which are added notes on Part I and strictures on Part II of The Pentateuch and book of Joshua

ISBN/EAN: 9783337733247

Printed in Europe, USA, Canada, Australia, Japan

Cover: Foto ©ninafisch / pixelio.de

More available books at **www.hansebooks.com**

BISHOP COLENSO ON THE PENTATEUCH,

QUOTED AND EXAMINED

TO WHICH ARE ADDED

NOTES ON PART I. AND STRICTURES ON PART II. OF THE PENTATEUCH AND BOOK OF JOSHUA.

BY THE
REV. JOHN STEPHEN, A.M.,
AUTHOR OF
"EXPOSITIONS ON THE ROMANS," "UTTERANCES OF THE CXIX. PSALM," ETC.

ABERDEEN:
ROBERT WALKER, 92, BROAD STREET;
EDINBURGH: JOHN MENZIES;
LONDON: HAMILTON, ADAMS, & CO.

1863.

CONTENTS.

		Bishop Colenso's Chapters.	Page.
INTRODUCTION	... ...	...	5
I. THE GENERATIONS.			
1. Judah's Family	... ...	ii., iii.	12
2. The Sojourning	... ...	xv.	15
3. The Fourth Generation	... ...	xvi.	18
II. EVENTS.			
4. The Passover	... ...	x. ...	22
5. March out of Egypt	... ...	xi. ...	24
6. Armed	... ...	ix. ...	28
III. PROVISION.			
7. Tents	... ...	viii. ...	29
8. The Desert	... ...	xii. ...	31
IV. NUMBER.			
9. Number at the Time of the Exodus		xvii., xix. ...	35
10. The Danites and Levites at the Exodus		xviii. ...	39
11. The Two Counts	... ...	vii. ...	42
12. The First-born	... ...	xiv. ...	45
V. EXTENT.			
13. The Court	... ...	iv.	50
14. The Law Read in the Hearing of all Israel		v.	52
15. Extent of Canaan	... ...	xiii.	55
VI. PRIESTS.			
16. The Camp	...	vi.	56
17. Duties	...	xx.	60
18. At the Passover		xxi.	64
VII. 19. War on Midian		xxii.	67
NOTES ON PART I. ...		...	73
STRICTURES ON PART II.		...	76

BISHOP COLENSO ON THE PENTATEUCH, QUOTED AND EXAMINED.

INTRODUCTION.

WHEN I heard of a Bishop of the Church of England stating objections in reference to the early records of Scripture, my expectation was to find raised difficulties as to the Creation, the Flood, the Dispersion, the passage of the Red Sea, the conduct of the Israelites through the wilderness under the pillar, the Jordan standing up as a heap, the Sun standing still at the command of Joshua; perhaps, more theologically, the descent of mankind from a single pair, the Fall, or some such doctrine or fact. But on opening the book, instead of that which I expected, I found, with no small degree of dislike to the subject, the dryest statistics, admeasurements, and objections, which might be classed as Numbers, Extent, and Impossibilities. The author might conscientiously have entertained doubts, on many such points, as to the correctness of the interpretations which have usually been put upon them; he goes farther than this, however, calling in question, indeed, the integrity of the Bible history, so setting at nought the internal evidence, the authenticity, and divine authority of the Book. He speaks as follows (Intro. p. 10) :—" I wish to repeat most distinctly, that my reason for no longer receiving the Pentateuch as historically true, is not that I find insuperable difficulties with regard to the *miracles*, or supernatural *revelations* of Almighty God, recorded in it, but solely that I cannot, as a true man, consent any longer to shut my eyes to the absolute, palpable, self-contradictions of the narrative." Yet, once his mind gave the most unhesitating assent to the voice of God as speaking in the Bible (p. 6). Now he seems to have got into a higher region than that of the Bible, for he says, p. 12, "Our belief in the Living God remains as sure as ever, though not the Pentateuch only, but the whole Bible, were removed." He will, therefore, take the Bible into his own hand. He says (p. 13), "Truth in the present instance is this, that the Pentateuch, as a whole, was not written by Moses, and that, with respect to some, at least, of the chief portions of the story, it cannot be regarded as historically true. The Bible does not, therefore, cease to 'contain the true Word of God,' with 'all things necessary for salvation,' to be 'profitable for doctrine, reproof, correction, instruction in righteousness.'"

Were the book before us not composed by a man in high official standing, a dignitary of the Church of England, I think, whatever might be the impression at first reading, the ultimate conclusion would be, that it would occasion little serious alarm in reflecting minds. In his Introductory part, the author speaks with great apparent candour, and no doubt thinks that he is candid; and magnanimous withal when he talks of giving up all in vindication of the truth; yet in course of reading, it becomes obvious that there is a degree of self-deception in his mind, and it might be added, a considerable haze in his intellectual vision. He wants discrimination, for he jumbles things together that ought to be kept separate—(p. 64, 124, 126, 129); he deals sometimes unfairly, assuming what is not generally maintained, as when he founds on the sojourn of 430 years (p. 97); he even doubts his own conclusions (p. 118, l. 1); yet such is his infatuation, that, once embrued in mischief, he goes on in the spirit of destructiveness, as if bent on removing the foundations of Bible belief. He finds consolation (xxxiii.) that the Court of Arches has declared, that what is meant in the Ordination Service for Deacons is, that "the Holy Scriptures contain everything necessary to salvation," and "to that extent they have the sanction of the Almighty." According to this, they may contain many things not to be believed.

It is not difficult to conceive, as he indicates himself, how he may have been led into this tendency of thinking. From childhood we, in this country, are taught to read the Bible history without question, till the mind become agreeably familiarised to it; whereas the position in which he found himself as a translator, having for his assistants men of subtle minds, who heard these things of Bible record in mature age for the first time, and started all manner of inquiries, was such that doubts which he entertained before rose to certainties, and the early predilections of the poor Bishop were overset.

We feel strongly inclined to know the history of a mind that, versed in learning, indoctrinated in the articles of the Church of England, and inspired by its high interests, should at any period allow itself to be swayed into misgivings that eventually overturn to itself the foundations of faith. It arises in one's thought, that more must be in such a mind than perplexities arising from apparent historical contradictions. Should we go to the depths of belief, and find unsoundness there, all would be explained. His exposition of the Epistle to the Romans certainly would let us into this—which yet I have not seen.

Single-hearted men may think they would set the matter in a fair light and satisfy the writer, by accounting for the apparent contradictions, and explaining the difficulties. Simple! The Bishop has made up his mind; they should look at the matter more seriously. They must abide by the essentials of their faith, which would be by these representations sapped; they must grasp the entire Word as we have it; and meantime rest, that He who gave the Word has provided the means whereby the difficulties which still in some degree cloud it, shall pass away, as many have done before.

Strange, notwithstanding, it is that a man of such mild and moderate sentiments as make up the book before us, should get into the rigid determination of destroying what he formerly revered. But mind may become wayward. He seems eager to seize objections against the credibility of the Mosaic history, introducing some that make very little to the purpose, as the size of the Court (iv.), dwelling in Tents (viii.), the Israelites

Armed (ix.), the Extent of Canaan (xiii.) When we consider what he advances on these, we are much relieved. Of the weight to be attached to his arguments where the subject appears more serious, we can judge by these. And we are led back to inquire, What can be his object? There must be some deep perversion which we do not see. I suspect he will measure doctrines as he measures things—the great doctrine of the atonement. I can only conceive that his mind has acquired such a bent that, not for onslaught, but truth, he determines on setting forth all of Old Testament history in the light of extravagance.

As we enter on the perusal of the book, we are startled by the statements, somewhat novel, yet not important in themselves. When we have considered the whole attentively, we suspect there is weakness in the premises, and wonder that a man of attainments should give place to trifling presentations, at the expense of all that should be dear to him. We may stumble because of the representations made, but we cannot give up our faith. We rather conclude that we have not sufficiently studied and understood. An attentive mind, submissive to the will of God, knowledge of ancient customs and religious practice, familiarity with the style of expression, acquaintance also with modern travel, are among the requisites to a right interpretation of Scripture. We abide by what we have been taught to revere as sacred. To the writings of Moses, as we now have them, collected by Ezra, according to tradition, on the return from Babylon, we have the highest attestation—that of our divine Lord. The Bishop's explanation (xxx.) of our Lord's reference to Moses (John v. 46; Luke xvi. 29; xx. 37; xxiv. 27, 44), that he referred only to *certain parts* of the Pentateuch, that he accommodated his words to the current language of the day, and that there is reason to ask, "Why should it be thought that He would speak with certain *Divine* knowledge on this matter, more than upon other matters of ordinary science or history?"—all this we must utterly repudiate. Our reason we must apply to the understanding of Scripture, but our reason we do not exalt above Scripture. We do not place Human Reason in the seat of Verity, to judge concerning all things—even concerning the averments of the Word; we place the Word there —" casting down imaginations, and every high thing that exalteth itself against the knowledge of God, and bringing into captivity every thought to the obedience of Christ."

Great evil will be through the province of Natal by such a man. The evil will take root, and will never likely be wholly eradicated. Ought not the Church of England to see to this? But he says (p. 139) the Church of England has had such things little before the mind. The Bishop of Clogher wrote on the Chronology of the Hebrew Bible a hundred years ago; Dr. Jennings has written at large on the Antiquities of the Jews; and the late Archbishop of Canterbury has given us an Essay on the Jewish Polity. We cannot but wonder what is the mind of Bishop Colenso himself, with regard to the object of his mission. For what has he gone to Natal? and why does he translate the Scriptures of the Old Testament, having such views? Is he actually employed upon Arabian Nights Entertainments?

From certain hints (p. 147), we are given to understand, that the writer foresees a modification, if not solution, of the difficulties, indefinite and imperfect even to himself. He will reduce the thousands of Israel to the dimensions of a travelling caravan, and contrive to lead them onward to Canaan, in a path not altogether devoid of the necessaries of life. So he will preserve the allusion to the journey found in the prophets, and the references in the gospels and epistles. All this time he is allowing himself the large liberty of selection. Forthwith he may come to doctrines, and let reason choose, as he obscurely hints in his concluding remarks. We shall then have reason set up with authority, as judge of the word of God; but to what does all this tend but the voice *ex cathedra* of "J. W. Natal?"

I read now, what I read in early life, the narration of Jehovah's doings among his ancient people. I recall the charm of those early impressions. Doubt entered not the mind. The truthfulness of the narrative, in its native simplicity, was all to the mind. God was believed to come down and talk with his people; and he led them in a right way amid their manifold rebellions, to bring them to the promised land. In dealing with this Publication, we are not called to take up the large field of Bible evidence, authenticated miracle, fulfilled prediction, the stream of attestation kept up, the whole internal evidence of divine authority. The Bishop does not expect this. He admits the general evidence; and only adventures to controvert a certain department of the internal evidence, viz., the integrity of the Bible History. He denies not miraculous interpositions where they are stated to be such; but where no such statement is made, he expects things to occur after the common course of events, and unless it be shown that they do so, he will take leave to deny the veracity of the history. We must meet him on this, his chosen battle-field. It is not enough to say, our divine Lord hath given his attestation to the Mosaic History; we must shew, in every instance where there is an absence of miracle—even an absence in the record—that events fall out according to the usual course of events. The man has this task before him that would attempt to convince the Bishop, whose subtle and studied statements shew us he is a man that will not be easily convinced.

The mind of Bishop Colenso on inspiration, we may infer from the manner in which he speaks of the sacred writers. The following are instances:—"We have already had reason to see that the statements of the chronicler are not always trustworthy" (p. 109). "It must now, surely, be sufficiently plain that the account of these numbers is of no statistical value whatever" (p. 111). "Which show that, in the prophet's view, at all events, such sacrifices were required and expected of them" (p. 123). Inferentially, he thus calls in question the whole word of God. Then, in his Preface (xxxi.) he speaks of our Lord as growing in wisdom like any other, and asks, "At what period, then, of his life upon earth is it to be supposed, that He had granted to Him, as the Son of Man, supernaturally, full and accurate information in these points, so that he should be expected to speak about the Pentateuch in other terms, than any other devout Jew of that day would have employed? Why should it be thought that He would speak with certain *Divine* knowledge on this matter, more than upon other matters of ordinary science or history?" Jesus did increase "in wisdom and stature, and in favour with God and man;" and it was when he entered on his divine ministry, that he was endued with the Holy Ghost above measure. But the Bishop of Natal will judge even of Christ's declarations. In short, as he counsels (p. 152), we must apply our human reason, and look for the sign of God's Spirit, speaking to us in the Bible, in that of which our own hearts alone can be the judges—in that which speaks to the witness for God within us—Reason and Conscience, to which alone, under God, each man is ultimately responsible. And this the Bishop will do, not that he does not reverence the Bible, but that he may take note from the inner man, and that nothing may be presented to the heathen mind that might cause offence. How would Paul, apostle to the Gentiles, have done had he followed this rule in Bible exposition? Reverence of the word of God is wanting here, which tells fearfully on the state of the mind. He quotes Scott with respect. How sound are the conclusions of Scott! a man that may not be reputed learned in comparison of the great prelates of England; and how came his sound conclusions? Laborious in the Word of God, his conclusions are the results of patient investigation by a mind chastened by the grace of God, through long and trying experiences.

NOTE.—It will be seen by the Contents, that I have not followed the arrangement adopted by Bishop Colenso. For the arrangement of subjects he has chosen, he has had his own reasons—no doubt to make his arguments bear all the better upon the design, as we are led to see on his introducing us to chapters xv., xvi., xvii., and xviii. of his book. The arrangement which I have chosen has reference to the specific—is according to the kinds of subject, which answer better to curtail the field of reasoning.

Dr. Colenso formally commences his objections to the Mosaic record, with his chapter on the Family of Judah. Some of the things to which he adverts in his Preface and Introduction, may be noticed in the conclusion of our Reply, in so far as they are worthy of notice, and shall not have been noticed in the course of remark; but, until the Bishop take them up formally, and exhibit his reasons for objecting to the Scripture statement, it were too much to reply, and furnish also the reasons of objection.

1.—JUDAH'S GRANDCHILDREN.

The first difficulty taken up in form concerns the family of Judah, and may be stated thus :

Judah, at the early age of 42 or 43, had grandchildren, who being also the grandchildren of Tamar, his daughter-in-law, were in descent equal to Judah's great-grandchildren.

By consulting the following passages, the above will appear: Gen. xxxviii.; Gen. xlvi. 8, 12, 26, 27 ; Ex. i. 1, 5 ; Deut. x. 22.

It would also appear that Asher and Benjamin have grandchildren named (v. 17 and v. 21, compared with Num. xxvi. 40); but this is not taken up in the way of difficulty and objection.

We have, then, to do with the descendants of Judah who are said to have come with Jacob into Egypt.

Bishop Clayton supposes that Jacob was married at the end of the first week (Gen. xxix.), which would remove the difficulty, were the supposition at all in accordance with the narrative.

We might, with more allowance, suppose, that there might have been years of interval before the years of great plenty came (Gen. xli. 45—47), during which Joseph went out over all the land of Egypt, making adequate preparation for the expected abundance (Gen. xli. 48, 49 ; xlvii. 13—22). It is frequent in Old Testament history, that intervals of longer or shorter duration take place which are not filled up in the narrative ; and, likewise, that the sequence of events is not always observed. The supposition above-made would not seem to be unreasonable when we consider all things. By a process of reckoning backward, from the statement which Jacob makes to Pharaoh of his years, we arrive at the conclusion that Jacob was about 75 in going to Padan-aram ; his mother, therefore, could be none less than 110, and her brother Laban would be more (Gen. xxii. 23 ; xxiv. 29, 50), all which seem inconsistent with the activities they display at subsequent periods (Gen. xxvii. ; xxx. ; xxxi.)

Most of the commentators, however, explain the difficulty as to Judah's family, that these, his grandchildren, though born in Egypt, came *in* their father, and that the limit is that of "heads" of families, which means that all were mentioned who became heads of families in Israel. This is not satisfactory; for some are mentioned here who are not found among the "heads," and many more are mentioned among the heads than are found here. (Compare with Num. xxvi.)

The narrative in Gen. xlvi. does seem to be given with marked precision, of which Bishop Colenso avails himself to an extreme degree; and yet we find that even in such details, there is a latitude that must be allowed in accordance with the style of ancient simplicity. Thus, including the birth of Benjamin, which took place in Canaan (Gen. xxxv. 18), we have an account of the family of Jacob, (Gen. xxxv. 22):—"Now the sons of Jacob were twelve. The sons of Leah—Reuben, Jacob's first-born, and Simeon, and Levi, and Judah, and Issachar, and Zebulon. The sons of Rachel—Joseph and Benjamin. And the sons of Bilhah, Rachel's handmaid—Dan and Napthali. And the sons of Zilpah, Leah's handmaid—Gad and Asher. These are the sons of Jacob, which were born to him in Padan-aram."

I have also observed, that we are not to assume, that every circumstance is put down consecutively as it occurred, and with due chronologic position as to its date. See the events of Jacob's life after his return to Canaan as a specimen—the birth of Benjamin and the death of Isaac recorded within a few verses of one another, though an interval of some twenty years had taken place; digressions concerning the families of Esau and of Judah; the birth of Er, and immediately almost his marriage. So here, in the catalogue of Jacob's family, though it be the record of their entering Egypt, it may have been made up years after. It has scope enough till the end of Jacob's life; several of those named in this catalogue may have been born in Egypt.

The enumeration in Gen. xlvi. seems to be a complete list of all Jacob's seed during his lifetime; and it serves as a first, though not perfect, list of the heads of families.

But how does all this agree with the repeated declaration, that these all came into Egypt with Jacob?

1. The expression—came with Jacob into Egypt—is used of the whole, as a whole, because it is true of the most. Besides the example given above in the instance of Benjamin, I may

refer to the genealogy of Esau's descendants in Gen. xxxvi., where children born to him in Canaan are said to be of "the generations of Esau, the father of the Edomites, in Mount Seir." As we say of a foreign family residing among us, though several of their children may have been born here, they come from such a country. Canaan was the home of Israel; so they would say of them at any period, they came from Canaan, and they return to Canaan.

2. Moreover, the expression—they all came with Jacob into Egypt—is over-strained. We read, verse 8, "And these are the names of the children of Israel which came into Egypt, Jacob and his sons; Reuben, Jacob's first-born." This verse seems to confine the names of those that came with Jacob into Egypt to Jacob's twelve sons; and then, as if each were named, as Reuben is, at the beginning, there is subjoined to each a list of the sons' or daughters' names. "And the sons of Reuben, &c.," (see Ex. i. 1—5). Similar to this is the style used in reference to the grandchildren, (v. 12), "And the sons of Pharez were Hezron and Hamul;" (v. 17), "And the sons of Beriah, Heber and Malchiel." Then as to the coming *with* Jacob, it is not positively expressed that all those, whose names are here came with, or in company with Jacob. Literally v. 26 expresses, "All the souls coming to Jacob to Egypt, those coming out of his loins, without Jacob's sons' wives, all the souls were threescore and six." The proposition, *le*, conveys the idea of property, or motion towards, and may be presented in its native indefiniteness—since Bishop Colenso insists so rigidly on literality, by the use of our preposition *to*. Moreover, as to the *coming* into Egypt, the expression is employed with much latitude as true of the family; not strictly of every individual member of it. As instances of this indefinite mode of expression, it may be noticed, that Jacob himself is counted among his descendants, (v. 15); and that Joseph and his two sons are said also to have come into Egypt (v. 27), "And the sons of Joseph, who were born to him in Egypt, were two souls; all the souls belonging to the house of Jacob, those coming into Egypt, were threescore and ten." (See also Ex. i. 5, and Deu. x. 22).

3. The form of expression, as partly seen from the last, does

not positively convey, that they—all the children mentioned—came together with Jacob—at the same time. What is conveyed, as noted above, is, that they belonged to him. The proper expression, signifying together with, in company of, is found in this chapter as elsewhere. *Yachad,* or more generally with a suffix, *yachdav,* or *yachdaiv* is the word signifying *together with,* (Gen. xiii. 6 ; xxii. 6, 8), which, however, does not occur in the present passage. But two others, pretty nearly conveying the same signification, occur, *eth* and *ghim,* signifying *with,* as, Gen. xxvii. 44., (ghimmo), xxix. 6, 7 (ghim), and here in chap. xlvi. v. 4, " I will go down with thee (ghimm' cha) into Egypt;" and Gen. xxx. 29 (itti) ; and xlvi. v. 6, " Jacob and his seed with him," (itto), and v. 7, " brought he with him" (itto). But in v. 26, the reading is different—" All the souls coming to Jacob to Egypt, (le yaghakob mitzraimah), those coming out of his loins, with Jacob's sons' wives, all the souls were threescore and six. And the sons of Joseph, which were born him in Egypt, were two souls : all the souls pertaining to the house of Jacob, those coming into Egypt, were threescore and ten."

But to all this it will be replied, and is replied by Bishop Colenso, How do you explain the marked distinction between Joseph's children and the rest, be it the case that some of the rest were born in Egypt ? Evidently the main distinction in the historian's mind was not the mere act of coming into Egypt, for he says, (v. 27), they all came. The distinction may be found herein, that Joseph had assumed a position in Egypt, so as to become the nourisher of his father and his father's family, which the sacred historian may be marking in the distinction he makes, and which, as it were, he immediately obliterates, by classing both families together in coming into Egypt.

II.—THE SOJOURNING.

I HAVE already referred to the strange inclination of such a man as a Bishop of the Church of England to introduce matter, weighing against the integrity of the sacred books, that is of little moment, and apparent discrepancies which he does not deem of any moment himself. The author's notes on the

Sojourning in Egypt (chap. xv.) exemplify the latter, and his notes on the Exodus, in the Fourth generation (chap. xvi), exemplify the former. Now, several respectable commentators admit, that the 430 years of sojourn date from the time of the calling of Abraham; yet the Bishop dwells at length upon the narrative as setting forth 430 years of sojourn in Egypt. He says the English translation does not decide the question; and is unusual and awkward in the expression—"Now the sojourning of the children of Israel, who dwelt in Egypt, was four hundred and thirty years" (Ex. xii. 40). He thinks the original words would be more naturally translated—"the sojourning of the children of Israel, *which they sojourned in Egypt*, &c." He should say it boldly, for it is far more agreeable to usage to understand the words thus : "Now the sojourning of the children of Israel, as to which they sojourned in Egypt, was four hundred and thirty years." Had all the time been meant, the simple form of expression would likely have been—"the sojourning of the children of Israel in Egypt." But construe the clauses, and we read thus—"the sojourning of the children of Israel, as to which they sojourned in Egypt"—and the fact conveyed is, that they sojourned 430 years, a portion of that period being in Egypt. Bishop Colenso, I suppose, would not obstinately reject this interpretation, but it would be a marvel if he did not think of saying, it could not be 'the children of Israel,' seeing there were no children of Israel in Abraham's days. It may be, however, that he will allow the generic name, "children of Israel," to extend back a little. To reconcile him also to the whole idea, he may recollect that the predecessors of Israel, Abraham and Isaac, both sojourned in Egypt in times of famine.

Throughout his two chapters, xv. and xvi., the Bishop's design is to curtail the time of the sojourn in Egypt, that he may prove the impossibility of there having been so great a number of men at the Exodus, as is stated to have been. He is, therefore, in earnest about the 430 years, that he may abbreviate them, and about the four generations, that he may hold to them. He brings in here, as several times elsewhere, the genealogical account of Levi's descendants (Ex. vi. 16—20), to shew, from even four lengthened lives, of Levi, Kohath, Amram,

Moses, that the period of sojourn could not have been 430 years. Some, however, suppose there were gaps in this line of descent; but it may be conceded that Bishop Colenso makes out his point well. He also deals with Kurtz, here and at p. 116, on the struggles which Kurtz makes to clear away this difficulty. Kurtz is equally strenuous for the 430 years, and uses all his skill to show how this period is reconcileable with the narrative. He finds the greatest difficulty in Jochebed, the daughter of Levi, being wife to Amram, his grandson, and being the mother of Aaron and Moses (Kurtz ii. 141). He goes even so far as to suppose a corruption in the passage Num. xxvi. 59; but whether that may arise from the explanatory clause, or the absence of the nominative (which is a common occurrence in Hebrew, Gen. ii. 20; Deut. xxxiv. 6) does not appear. The explanation is, to adopt the text as it stands, and to admit the abbreviated period of 215 years of sojourn in Egypt.

I conceive that the period of sojourn, with regard to the *where* the sojourn took place, is decisively settled by the Apostle Paul, who, in the Galatians (chap. iii. 16, 17), dates it from the time of the calling of Abraham, and particularly of indicating to him the covenant as the type of Christ (Gen. xv.) So, indeed, we read, v. 13, "And he said unto Abraham, Know of a surety that thy seed shall be a stranger in a land which is not theirs, and shall serve them; and they shall afflict them four hundred years. . . . But in the fourth generation they shall come hither again; for the iniquity of the Amorites is not yet full."

This period of about 430 years is remarkable in the history of Jehovah's people. With a little variation, it will be found to obtain in the following periods, viz., from Noah to Abraham, and from Abraham to the Exodus, and from the Exodus to David, and from David to Zedekiah: from Zedekiah to Christ is considerably more.

We allow, then, that the 430 years of sojourn commences with the time of Jehovah entering into covenant with Abraham, as the type of him who was to come; and, of course, that the period appertaining to Egypt was 215 years.

III.—THE EXODUS IN THE FOURTH GENERATION.

I HAVE referred above to chapter xvi. of the Bishop's book, which deals on the Exodus in the Fourth Generation. Perversely, on the one hand, he maintains the plea of absurdity in the chronology of the narrative, reckoning still by the 430 years ; and, then, on the other, assuming the period to have been 215 years, he reckons by only four generations, to show how impossible it is that there could have been a progress of population able to furnish 600,000 able men. He will not look to the fact, that the "four generations" were leading generations of four lengthened lives. Possibly the "four generations" meant, and the 430 years of sojourn, may be the same period— 100 years each generation—which will be in the Bishop's favour, although it throw him out of his count. We shall enter more minutely into this important distinction when we come to speak on the Numbers at the time of the Exodus. Meantime, the Bishop should know that, be the "four generations" what they may, there were 215 years of sojourn in Egypt, and that in 215 years there would be of ordinary generations seven, in place of four, for from many instances it appears, that the common generations, as to issue, ran much as they do now, at periods of 30 years.

But the Bishop is jealous to a degree on this point. It might be surmised that, in looking over this part of the subject, he came upon Gen. l. 23, and read, to his discomfort, "And Joseph saw Ephraim's children of the third generation : the children also of Machir, the son of Manasseh, were brought up upon Joseph's knees." This must have cost him many a thought ; for it was a complete overthrow to his scheme of four generations during the sojourn, to be confronted with four even in Joseph's time, when only 70 years of the sojourn were expired. But what will a desperate man not do? He knew there were other lists of names and pedigrees in the Bible history, and at last, we may suppose, he stumbled upon 1 Chron. vii. 22—27, where he found a morsel to his mind. In this passage we have the list of Joshua's ancestors, and find nine generations. Hereupon the Bishop remarks, this is an exception to the prevailing rule obtaining in the Pentateuch. So briefly he avers, we have nothing to do with the Chronicles on a question in the Pentateuch. We wonder, then, why he adverts to the Chronicles. Yet, notwithstanding, he returns to say, that the Chronicles exhibit the rule of the Pentateuch in other cases, and that this is the single exception.

And he proceeds to analyse this statement in Chronicles, showing that between the birth of Telah, the great-grandson of Ephraim, and that of Joshua, 100 years, there must have been six complete generations. Put the case more simply thus: during the 215 years, there were nine generations in the line of Ephraim. This is simply unusual, but not incredible, as the Bishop would aver. In chapter xv. of his book, he was concerned to make out, that there were not 430 years of sojourn, but only 215; now, in his xvi., he is concerned to make out, that there were but *four* generations in the 215 years of sojourn. Hence his attempt to break down the account of Joshua's descent as given in Chronicles. He then, out of the same line of Ephraim, would fain make something of Elishama, the grandfather of Joshua, being captain of the host of Ephraim. He would make it out that this was incredible also. But Caleb was a leader of Israel when equally old (Josh. xiv. 11), and continued so. Later than this, Joshua, contemporary with Caleb, continued leader of all Israel.

But Bishop Colenso knows not when to have done with objecting. He pursues the theme in the same line of family. He states the matter thus: But in truth, the account of Joshua's descent in 1 Chron. vii. involves a palpable contradiction. Thus, in v. 24, we are told, that Ephraim's daughter built two villages in the land of Canaan. If we suppose this to mean that the *descendants* of Ephraim's daughter, after the conquest in the time of Joshua, did this, yet, in v. 22, 23, we have this most astonishing fact stated, that Ephraim himself, after the slaughter by the men of Gath of his descendants in the *seventh* generation, "mourned many days," and then married again, and had a son, Beriah, who was the ancestor of *Joshua!* This Beriah, however, is not named at all among the sons of Ephraim in the list given in Num. xxvi. 35. This is the Bishop's representation of the case; and the pains he has taken to demolish the argument for more than four generations during the sojourn, founded upon the descent of Joshua as given in Chronicles, must be very obvious. It is a life and death matter with him to destroy it; hence the extravagant representations given above. He would admit that it was a descendant of Ephraim's daughter that built two villages in Canaan after its conquest by Joshua, certainly not to waive the absurdity of Ephraim's own daughter doing it in the time of Joshua, but to keep up the equal absurdity of a long line of seven generations of a first family, and then nine generations of a second, both of Ephraim. But he makes the unwarrantable supposition that Ephraim's daughter built the villages after the conquest of Canaan by Joshua, and the still more unwarrantable supposition that it was after seven generations of the first family that he had Beriah, the first of the second series of generations.

Now, the whole reckoning of these families depends upon the interpretation of the terms in which the facts are conveyed. Bishop Colenso quotes Kuenen to the effect, that when the words occur *and his son*, they signify an additional son of the father last spoken of, and a brother of the last son mentioned; whereas, when the words *his son* occur, they signify a descendant farther down, son of the last-mentioned son. According to this rule, the sons mentioned in 1 Chron. vii. 20, 21, would be all sons of Ephraim and brothers to one another. Also, the sons mentioned in v. 23, 25, would also be his sons and brothers to one another; while (v 26, 27) Laadan would be the son of Tahan, Ammihud the son of Laadan, Elishama the son of Ammihud, Non the son of Elishama, and Joshua the son of Non. Thus Joshua would be the sixth from Ephraim. In opposition to this, Dr. Colenso mentions three objections, the third being only an explanation. The second is, that, in two instances, two of the family bear the same name, which would be improper to our modern ideas, but not so in those early times, when names bore significations. His first objection is presented thus: I point to 1 Chron. ix. 43, "*and* his son Rephaiah," compared with the parallel passage viii. 37, "his son Rapha." This is remarkably modest; the Bishop avoids committing himself by an opinion, even to the extent of a conjunction. He gives the conjunction, even italicised, but he only gives it. He puts it down, like an evil omen, that we may look at it and be silenced; but he says not what is the force of it. The same caution may be observed in all his references to the Original. A man who deals so unscrupulously with the Bible history deserves to be dealt with severely according to his merits. But to resume. Probably the better rule would be, to distinguish when the *Vau* couples names and when it couples members of sentences. When it couples names, it serves very much as above; but we are liable to mistake, applying it to genealogies (as in 1 Chron. vii. 25), when it only couples members of a sentence, which is really the case in Dr. Colenso's exception of 1 Chron. ix. 43.

Colenso's *seven* generations have now vanished, and his nine generations have diminished to six—the reasonable calculation; but it is not to be admired that, while he had suspicion of all this, he should make such a handle of it in argument. Moreover, the incidents referred to in 1 Chron. vii. 21, 22, 24, may probably amount to this, that while the Israelites sojourned in Egypt, incursions were made into Canaan, which were returned from the other side; and that men of Gath, born in the land (not naming which) slew of the sons of Ephraim when they (indefinite) came down to take away their cattle. Then, during the same sojourn, Sherah, the daughter of Ephraim, may have begun the villages mentioned (v. 24). Some respected commentators, taking a different view, understand this Sherah to have been a descendant of Ephraim, which fails to harmonise with the interpretation given above. So far, however, as concerns the main point—viz., the *generations*, Bishop Colenso's attempt requires only to be examined in order to be exposed.

The subject of the Sojourn, and especially of the Generations, will be resumed when we come to speak of the Number at the time of the Exodus—Art. IX.

IV.—INSTITUTION OF THE PASSOVER.

WE come to consider what is said in this book, concerning the Keeping of the Passover, and the March out of Egypt (chap. x. and xi.), having considered the Sojourning and the Four Generations. Both the Keeping of the Passover, and the March out of Egypt, are represented in the light of impossibility; and both presenting similar difficulties, require to be met similarly. I confine attention, meantime, to the Keeping of the Passover. *In one single day*, it is affirmed in this book, the immense multitudes were instructed to keep the Passover, and did actually keep it, such is the history. And on what does the Bishop found this affirmation? On the simple words *this night*—" For I will pass through the land of Egypt this night, and will smite all the first-born in the land of Egypt, both man and beast, and against all the gods of Egypt I will execute judgment: I am the Lord" (Ex. xii. 12). And, again, the words *about midnight*—" And Moses said, thus saith the Lord, About midnight will I go out into the midst of Egypt. And all the first-born in the land of Egypt shall die" (Ex. xi. 4). He also refers to "this day" (v. 14). It is added, there can be no doubt that the "midnight" next at hand is intended. And upon this simple basis the Bishop rears the charge of an impossibility, recorded in the narrative. In one day, all the heads of Israel were instructed in the Keeping of the Passover, and on the night of that day, all the heads did keep it in their families. And all this proceeded from one man, who was himself instructed in the same day. "Speak ye unto all the congregation of Israel, &c." (Ex. xii. 3). "Then Moses called for all the elders of Israel, and said unto them, Draw out, and take you a lamb, according to your families, and kill the Passover" (v. 21). Then the Bishop takes pains to show the extent of space which so great a number must have occupied, and how impossible it would have been on any supposition to communicate in so brief a time; and, verily when a man is bent upon making out an absurdity in any narration, means are ready to an ingenious mind. He goes first upon the *borrowing*, which implies proximity, to show, that if the Israelites lived along with the Egyptians in one city—say Rameses—that city must have been as large as London now is. Then abandoning this supposition, he reckons by the number of their small cattle, of which he forms an estimate from the 150,000 lambs they would, upon calculation, require for the observing of the Passover, that they would occupy a region as great as one of the large counties of England. Then the impossibility of communicating, in one day, minute instructions to all the heads of families, or, indeed, making any communication at all, over so great a space, is easily perceived. The difficulty advanced is this, How could the instructions about Keeping the Passover, and being ready to move at a given moment, be communicated in so short a space of time; and, finally, how were they to prepare and keep the Passover, and know the very moment at which they were all to start.

Now all this is said to have been done; and the Bishop says, it is an impossibility.

Without following him into all the absurdity of his manifold suppositions, we shall return to his premises—the basis of his argument—*this night—about midnight.* And he is serious on this point, for he says, it is "this," not "that,"—*this night.*

Turning to the instructions (chap. xii.) we read (v. 3), " Speak ye unto all the congregation of Israel, saying, In the tenth day of this month, they shall take to them every man a lamb . . . . (v. 6), And ye shall keep it up until the fourteenth day of the same month." Hereby they were all to be prepared at least four days before the great occasion. Also in order to take to them every man a lamb on the tenth, they must have had due warning. We are thus at liberty to go back to the first day of the month. But, further, the words (v. 2) "This month shall be unto you the beginning of months," do not absolutely convey the import that the month was come, but may otherwise signify the time referred to in the previous chapter, where the Israelites are directed to prepare for their departure by borrowing, and where the Lord says, "About midnight will I go out into the midst of Israel. And all the first-born in the land of Egypt shall die." And as for the Bishop's *this night* and *about midnight,* he seems to be oblivious of the familiar mode of composition, that past events, and future events, become often present in lively or striking narration. He can see things only with one eye, combined views being inadmissible ; and he can apply expression only in strict literality.

These are the minor, and more immediate indications, of preparation which have been taken up at present ; the general and comprehensive will be considered under the March out of Egypt. The narratives of sacred writ we cannot but revere from early associations ; feeling shocked upon finding them rudely and remorselessly assailed. But it is surprising that a man of mind and erudition should employ trivialities, such as he does employ, to make out a case before reflecting men—men deeply in favour too—against the veracity of the Bible history. He seems committed to the task of finding all manner of objections to the Bible record, which can be accounted for only on some supposition of his mind being already almost hopelessly prejudiced against the Bible history, as if there was an antagonism in the mind itself. So in place of entering into the beautiful simplicity of the Old Testament style, and receiving the scenes and facts which it presents in historic vision, he takes up the words and the expressions, one by one, and measuring them by his modern limited perceptions, pronounces upon them to the effect that they are unworthy of reception.

V.—THE MARCH OUT OF EGYPT.

IMMEDIATELY, as containing similar objections to the last, (x. the Passover), we come to the chapter (xi.) on the March out of Egypt. The objections are these : two millions of young and old, of both sexes, spread over a considerable extent of country, are summoned to start at a moment's notice, and are actually started, with their numerous flocks and herds. Suddenly at midnight, they gather their cattle, and having borrowed from the Egyptians what they required,—which would show that they were far spread, if they lived among the Egyptians, or had far to go, if they lived apart, they journeyed on, converging towards Rameses, the common place of rendezvous, carrying all with them, sick and infirm, aged and infants, effects and all. This is the impossibility. But, further, we see them now on their march, a multitude so great that, with fifty abreast, it will extend over a space of twenty-two miles in length, and many more if we include the cattle, the rear requiring two days to come up to the place of the van, so that, on the one supposition, it was impossible for all of them to have started from Rameses and reached Succoth, in one day, and impossible for them, on any supposition, to find provender for the cattle during the progress to Succoth, and then to Etham, and thence, on the third day, to the Red Sea. The same impossibility is presented in their march three days into the wilderness beyond the Red Sea, the writer heaping up objections in confusion of mind, or wantonly to destroy the credibility of the narrative.

These objections all rest upon the erroneous basis, the extraordinary assertion, that all was begun and ended in one night—the keeping of the Passover, the assembling at Rameses, and the progress to Succoth. The Bishop might have strengthened his position by saying that the Hebrews could not move till the order came from the king, and we read that Pharoah gave the order at midnight (Ex. xii. 31). Already this objection of the one night has been disposed of; but here I might ask, Had not the children of Israel been taught all along to expect a great deliverance? "And it came to pass in process of time, that the king of Egypt died; and the children of Israel sighed by reason of the bondage, and they cried: and their cry came up unto God, by reason of the bondage. And God heard their groaning, and God remembered his covenant with Abraham, with Isaac, and with Jacob. And God looked upon the children of Israel, and God had respect unto them" (Ex. ii. 23—25, comp. with Gen. xv. 7, 13—16; xviii. 5—8). Were they not brought into the immediate expectation of this by the arrival of Moses and Aaron (chap. iii. 8, 16, and iv. 29)? And as the time drew on they were more prepared (chap. xi. 2). They had been directed to borrow of the Egyptians beforehand, and Bishop Colenso would leave it to be thought that they also borrowed that night. Then, as we have seen, they were fully prepared to expect the great deliverance on the night of the *fourteenth*. Could they be otherwise than in readiness to the utmost extent of their power?

and every exertion would be put forth. And as for signal to move, the death of the first-born simultaneously, over all the land, was an awful signal to the Egyptians to be "urgent upon the people, that they might send them out of the land in haste ; for they said, We be all dead men."

Farther, because it is said, " And the children of Israel journeyed from Rameses to Succoth, about six hundred thousand on foot that were men, besides children. And a mixed multitude went up with them : and flocks and herds, even very much cattle " (Ex. xii. 37, 38), the Bishop assumes that, in the one night, all the people, dwelling in the different parts of Goshen, assembled at Rameses, and reached Succoth, a distance of perhaps 30 miles, ere the night following. This latter they might strain to do in the urgent circumstances, did they all start from the same place at the same time ; but what necessity was there for the greater part dwelling in Goshen to pass Succoth on the way to Rameses, and then having reached Rameses, to retrace their course in order to reach Succoth, as must be the case if our maps give any like a fair representation of country ? They are said to start from Rameses, because it was the main place, but naturally all would bend to the point of nearest contact with the advancing van, where Moses and Aaron were leading. The literal suppositions that none could join the advancing line at the nearest point unless he passed through Rameses, and that none could be said to have started until he went out there, is simply ridiculous. Besides, the name Rameses extends to a "land" (Gen. xlvii. 11), as well as to some principal city.

The Bishop proceeds, " And now let us see them on the march itself." The immense column is supposed to be in length twenty-two miles. The last of the body cannot start till the foremost have advanced twenty-two miles, which would require two days. So he says ; by which we understand that the foremost must be twenty-two miles on before the hindmost have reached Rameses, the place of starting. They only start there, though they may have come twenty, or thirty, or forty miles before. Now all must have come to Rameses and thence to Succoth, on the one day, he says ; whereas all that can be understood is, that those that set out first from Rameses might reach Succoth by night of that day ; the rest following in succession as they were able. The Bishop will not allow that they left Egypt on that night at all, unless they all left. He is particular in quoting Ex. xii. 31—41, 51, the last verse being, " And it came to pass the self-same day, that the Lord did bring the children of Israel out of the land of Egypt by their armies " —that certainly was the date of their being led out of Egypt. He also asserts it to be recorded that on the same day they reached Succoth. and thence, through Etham, the Red Sea on the third day, and we know that Moses asked three days (Ex. v. 3 ; viii. 27). But where is the mention of one day in reaching Succoth ? and where is the mention of three in reaching the Red Sea ?—the distance from Succoth to Etham, and from Etham to Pi-hahiroth, being greater than their first from Rameses to Succoth.

All at once the Bishop changes the form of argument, and demands, What did the two millions of sheep and oxen live upon during this journey from Rameses to Succoth, and from Succoth to Etham, and from Etham to the Red Sea ?" He continues the same question as to the three days from the Red Sea into the wilderness of Shur. We shall come to the question of food for the cattle in his next chapter ; but, meantime, we may retaliate, Where did the men find food ? which he allows.

Let us imagine that a well-designed map of the route supposed to have been pursued by the Israelites in their flight from Egypt is spread out, and that a few of those Zulu of Dr. Colenso's assistants are comparing this account of his with the map. The men smile to one another at the ridiculous suppositions which their Teacher has wrought out of the simple narrative, and marvel at European folly. They consider the instructions concerning the keeping of the first Passover, and conceive something of the solemn import, while their Bishop is amusing himself with questions as to how the instructions were given, and how the note of moving was conveyed. The men think, and conceive the whole.

The Israelites have partaken of the paschal feast ; they sit trembling in their habitations. The Bishop asks how the signal to move was conveyed. Hark! there is the cry of lamentation all around. In every habitation of the Egyptians there is the first-born dead—struck down by an invisible hand. This was the signal note, and immediately the Egyptians are urgent with them to be gone. Israel's God is present in anger, because of their detention; and the alarmed Egyptians implore them to take away the cause of anger with their presence. "And Pharoah rose up in the night, he, and all his servants, and all the Egyptians; and there was a great cry in Egypt: for there was not a house where there was not one dead. And he called for Moses and Aaron by night, and said, Rise up, and get you forth from among my people, both ye and the children of Israel and go, serve the Lord, as ye have said."

Forthwith, the whole of Israel is in motion. Rameses is the place named for starting, and onward they move by Rameses, or the nearest line of direction, towards the Red Sea, passing Succoth, and then Etham, thinking, no doubt, they had a straight course over, on the way to the promised Canaan, when all at once they are directed to turn down along the Red Sea—the pillar of cloud by day, and the pillar of fire by night, guiding their route, till they reach an estuary of the sea, Pi-hahiroth—the opening of the Hiroth—having the estuary in front, the Red Sea on one hand, and mountain rocks on the other, and anon the host of Pharoah behind them.

They were placed in a position where no human power was of avail. But we read, "And the children of Israel went out with a high hand" (Ex. viv. 8; Num. xxxiii. 3).

VI.—ARMED.

THE Bishop's notes on the Israelites Armed (chap. ix.), only strike us in one sense. We see his eagerness to gather up objections. His objections here are two—Where did they obtain their armour? and, Why, armed, were the 600,000 afraid? Pharoah would never have allowed such a body of men to possess armour; therefore, How did they possess it on leaving? And again, if armed, it is incredible that 600,000 men in the prime of life, having their wives and children to defend, should have been so panic-struck at the sight of Pharoah and his host. He adds, they showed no such fear when Amalek came down upon them. Such things have been: the armour might have been secretly provided, for that they possessed some kind of armour may be conceded; and as for fear, what more common than to find the same men and the same army afraid at one time and bold at another. In the Essay prefixed to Pope's "Homer," this trait is noticed in the heroes. The battle of Pharsalia will afford an instance of an army.

The point, however, like many others, I am sorry to observe, is strained. The original term is rendered *armed* very commonly; and there is little given anywhere to decide its special character; it stands simply as an adjective, signifying being in an attitude or condition for war, but by no means expressing any particular kind of preparation. One passage is quoted, however, which seems to give the precise import more than any other—(Judges vii. 11). Literally, Then went he down with Phurah his servant to the extreme of *the ranks* that were in the camp. Whence the whole matter is left in dubiety.

VII.—TENTS.

HIS chapter (viii.) on Tents is also of minor importance. Two objections are presented—How did the Israelites acquire such an enormous number of tents as were needed? and, How did they carry them? He still goes upon the footing of there being no time, no preparation. Unless all matters recorded in ancient history can be satisfactorily accounted for to this African Bishop, he will not receive them as true. Save time be given for due preparation, oxen to draw waggons of provision, stores of water and grass by the way, resting-places at proper stages, this Overseer of the flock of God will not set out. The Israelites went on faith. Indeed, this was one main branch of their forming a history, that they might teach God's people to walk by faith. The whole reasoning of this writer would seem to proceed upon the supposition also, that the Israelites were incapable of action and of the arts of human existence, and void of all materials wherein the arts are employed. So simple were they, that they had not even attained the art of tent-making. Certainly, there could have been little difficulty in their providing materials, or even acquiring them at the latest, so urgent were the Egyptians to be delivered from the impending wrath; and there could have been little difficulty in carrying or drawing them. The father and sons of one family might carry or convey the simple apparatus of one tent, with whatever else was necessary; and a thousand families could do the same.

He finds a difficulty in Lev. xxiii. 42, 43, "Ye shall dwell in booths seven days; all that are Israelites born shall dwell in booths; that your generations may know that I made the children of Israel to dwell in booths, when I brought them out of the land of Egypt: I am the Lord your God." He says the statement of their dwelling in tents conflicts strangely with the charge that they should dwell in booths. One part of the narrative conflicts with another. So he avers, and leaves an adverse inference to be drawn. The one part does not conflict with the other. The use of tents was common all the year; the dwelling in booths for seven days in the year, was intended to teach them their temporary sojourn in this world. So was it commanded to be continued throughout their generations (Deut. xvi. 16).

On this subject of the Tents and the Booths, some remarks are called for. No doubt there was a difference in the materials and construction of these temporary ancient habitations. They were the habitations of the wilderness, and are not unfrequent at the present day. We read of booths among Indian tribes; and as for tents, they are familiar as our readings of modern travel and adventure. These two dwellings mentioned were no doubt different in kind, and the Bishop is anxious to show that there is conflict in the passages which speak of the children of Israel dwelling in both during their abode in the wilderness. The booth is mentioned, Gen. xxxiii. 17; and in Lev. xxiii. 40, the kind of it is particularised. We have descriptions of the tent in divers places (Gen. xxvi. 17; xxxv. 21; Ex. xxvi. 11; xxxv. 11). Had there been two names for one kind of thing, the Bishop would find the passages that speak about it all consistent; but there having been two things or kinds of temporary dwelling, he finds conflict in the passages. Now one would think he would rather have discovered great beauty in the very distinction between the things. Were it an order of divine authority that the prelates of England and her dependencies should forsake their palace habitations, and for a week or eight days be content with an humble booth for their habitation, would not this be a salutary lesson to pride? The tent was all the permanent habitation that Israel had in the wilderness of many years' sojourn and wandering; but they were required to forego even this sober kind of habitation, and take up with the more humble and even natural habitation of booths for seven days, that they might learn and teach the humbling and salutary fact of man's being a stranger and pilgrim in this world. The booths taught the lesson specially for the season, though, indeed, the tents taught it all the year through. The same was to be to them a perpetual statute, and so would they ever learn the lesson of faith. By faith he (Abraham) sojourned in the land of promise, as in a strange country, dwelling in tabernacles with Isaac and Jacob, the heirs with him of the same promise: for he looked for a city which hath foundations, whose builder and maker is God (Heb. xi. 9, 10).

VIII.—THE DESERT.

The Bishop insists that since there was no provision, of a miraculous kind for the cattle, as for the people, the history is improbable. The insinuation conveyed is, that it is untrue. Now mark the necessary inference: the Israelites did not pass such a journey, the Bible account of the numbers and the wanderings being fabulous. And, further, our Lord's admission of the miraculous supply of manna (John vi. 32, 49), and the doctrine shown forth therefrom of the Bread of Life (v. 35, 50), are vain. You would think that a man of the Bishop's penetration would have paused, when he could not but discern the fearful consequences to which his representations were tending.

Bishop Colenso fully admits of miracles, as to the Israelites themselves. The Passage of the Red Sea, the guidance of the pillar, the thunders of Sinai heard, water miraculously supplied, manna rained down—a special providence as to the people, he does not controvert, because such is declared in the narrative; but as to the cattle, he demands to know whence they were supplied with provender, his reason for insisting on this being, that no mention of miracle is made in reference to them.

If faith might speak, it would reply, He who provided for the people, would also provide for their cattle. Appointing animals for sacrifice and food (Lev. xvii.), he would provide for their sustenance in the desolate wild, into which he had brought the Israelites.

But strange to tell, a Bishop of the Church of England draws the most dreary discription of the wilderness and their wanderings that he can find, and because no mention is made of provender for the sheep and herds, rashly speaks of the impossibility of such a multitude of human beings existing. Whence he is prepared to teach that no such number of human beings ever traversed these wilds, and that the 600,000 are a fiction.

Throughout the subsequent books of Scripture, frequent reference is made to the early history of Israel, as detailed in these books of Moses—(1 Sam. xv.; Ps. cv., cvi., cvii.; Isa. lxiii.; Jer. ii.) The Jews were remarkable for their reverential regard of the sacred books, and in the collecting of them, and the preserving of them, as the Word of Jehovah, they knew that they were jealously watched by their neighbours the Samaritans, so far as the Pentateuch was concerned, which is the main part at present in question. Then frequent reference to the Old Testament Scriptures is found in the Gospels (not to repeat our Lord's attestation), and in the Epistles to the Galatians and the Hebrews. These stamp the early books with divine impressions, so that all must stand or fall together. Then these books of the Hebrew prophet speak for themselves in the fulfilment of the awful predictions contained therein. They came attested by miracles of which we have authentic record, and they continue to speak in wonderful fulfilments. They speak to the inner nature of man in convincing strain, which is the best kind of internal evidence; but since we are dealing on testimony and attestation, here are a living people to testify and attest. The descendants of that ancient people still independently exist, who, from age to age, have preserved with reverential care these sacred writings of antiquity, and who bearing witness to the supreme esteem in which these writings have ever been held, are themselves an awful fulfilment of the predictions pronounced by Moses on them, should they become disobedient (Deut. xxviii.) One singular testimony, verified by the apostle Peter, I shall quote—" How goodly are thy tents, O Jacob! and thy tabernacles, O Israel! As the valleys are they spread forth, as gardens by the river's side, as the trees of lign-aloes, which the Lord hath planted, and as cedar-trees beside the waters. He shall pour the water out of his buckets, and his seed shall be in many waters; and his king shall be higher than Agag, and his kingdom shall be exalted. God brought him forth out of Egypt; he hath, as it were, the strength of an unicorn; he shall eat up the nations his enemies, and shall break their bones, and pierce them through with his arrows. He couched, he lay down as a lion, and as a great lion; who shall stir him up? Blessed is he that blesseth thee, and cursed is he that curseth thee" (Num. xxiv. 5—9).

I may, however, give one answer in the Bishop's own vein, admitting all that is said of the "waste howling wilderness," and that around Sinai, except when awful revelations took place, as the Israelites stood in the Wady Mousa amid the thunders, there hovered a loneliness that was appalling.

Having tarried about a year around the precincts of Sinai and Horeb, the Israelites were then led forward into the open desert of Paran, where without miraculous supply they would find it impossible to subsist. Then, if you trace their course back, and all the turnings and windings of their devious route, through the desert of Zin, having the deep valley of El Ghor as its north entrance, and that of El Araba as its south, and then skirting round towards the eastern, or great stony desert, you will find that keeping close to the mountain ranges of mount Seir and other countries, long stripes of verdure and woodland were in their path. These stripes might extend a hundred miles, and be in some places twenty miles broad. Along these mountain ranges were powerful nations, Amalekites and Edomites, Midianites and Moabites, the kings of Heshbon and Bashan, whose great and small cattle must have had plenty of supply. Then to all this we have to add, parties of the 600,000 might go abroad, and range everywhere for the required provender. The fear of Israel was upon all the surrounding countries of their wanderings. Because no mention is made of provender; therefore there was none. Such is the Bishop's reasoning, who must have read Alison to little purpose, though he quotes him, else he would have found that, ample in detail as that writer commonly is, he thinks it unnecessary always to mention all the appendages of an army on the march, in battle, or in camp.

I have acknowledged the wild and barren character of those large regions of Arabia through which the Israelites passed. As we read, description after description of rocky, dry, leafless country meets our view. We have, however, to remember that even yet, on many accounts, the country of Arabia has been very imperfectly explored, and we have this to add, upon good authority, that there is reason to believe, the country may have deteriorated, both from natural causes, and the ruthless hand of the Beduin tribes. Of Araby the Blessed, we have not here to say, as Milton, that the seamen as they pass the southern seas are regaled by the balmy airs which are wafted from its shores. We have not much to say of even Arabia Deserta, for the route of the Israelites did not lie much there. Arabia the Rocky was the chief scene of their wanderings, and of it, as it is commonly marked in geography, we have spoken as containing the long verdant stripes that might scantily supply their cattle with food. I have turned up the names of the principal places mentioned in their wanderings in the "Imperial Gazetteer," where we have a condensed summary of manifold descriptions, and believe I am borne out in what I have said. It is singular, too, that even at this late age of the world, we may arrive at a satisfactory knowledge of what was the general aspect of these countries in ancient times. We read concerning Esau (Gen. xxxvi. 4—8), that he left Canaan, and went with all his family and numerous flocks and herds into Mount Seir, because Canaan was not able to sustain the brothers together in their mighty wealth of cattle. We may also recall that Moses led his father-in-law's flock round to the very peninsula where Sinai and Horeb stand like giants of the earth, and entitle it to the same name as the wonderful city of the Edomites. Certainly, the whole place may be called the mountain rock, with its mighty base of 60 and 70 miles. Round hither Moses led the flock, even to Mount Horeb, little imagining the terrific grandeurs that were there to transpire ; and little thinking that he was learning to be the leader of Israel in these very wilds. And here he must have found herbage for his flocks. Then away far from this scene, yet not distant from the time, we have account of another extraordinary man, Job, who lived in the land of Uz, probably in the north of Arabia Deserta, whose "substance was seven thousand sheep, and three thousand camels, and five hundred yoke of oxen, and five hundred she-asses, and a very great household ; so that this man was the greatest of all the men of the east" (Job i. 3). But, probably, should the Bishop cast his eye upon such passages as these in the early history, they will share the fate of the general history, and be called *unhistorical*, in the face of modern discovery, which hitherto has only penetrated to the outside and surface of the matter. I am afraid the Bishop must be transported back to the times of antiquity, and to the very places of the route pursued by Israel under the pillar ; and even though he were, he might, for the maintenance of his theory, deny the testimony of his own senses.

IX.—NUMBER AT THE EXODUS.

On the number of Israelites at the time of the Exodus, the Bishop finds insuperable difficulties. I am sorry that several respectable commentators seem too ready to admit great difficulty, and to labour to overcome it. 600,000 men are stated to have gone up from Egypt, which implies a population of 2,000,000. The Bishop is willing to make full allowance for longevity and increase, but he cannot find that the families then were much larger than they are now. He assumes that the 12 sons of Jacob had 53 sons, and no more, which is on an average 4½ each ; and that they increased in this ratio through *four* generations. By this rule, we have 4,923 instead of 600,000 warriors in the prime of life.

He then finds it necessary to diminish even this number, by supposing as many daughters as sons. Hereupon he draws the astounding conclusion, founded on the Scripture statement of 600,000 men, that each man had 46 children of both sexes (p. 116). Note.—His calculation in the case of the First-born is still more extraordinary. See chapter xiv.

From the manner in which he treats the Scripture record, I cannot suppose that the declarations in Ex. i. 7, 9, will have much weight with him :—" And the children of Israel were fruitful, and increased abundantly, and multiplied, and waxed exceeding mighty; and the land was filled with them. Now there arose up a new king over Egypt, which knew not Joseph. And he said unto his people, Behold the people of the children of Israel are more and mightier than we." The divine interposition is also declared (Gen. xlvi. 31), " And he said, I am God, the God of thy father ; fear not to go down into Egypt ; for I will there make of thee a great nation." So is the offerer taught to speak (Deut. xxvi. 5), ." And thou shalt speak and say before the Lord thy God, A Syrian ready to perish was my father ; and he went down into Egypt, and sojourned there with a few, and became there a nation, great, mighty, and populous."

The ratio of increase which the Bishop admits, but hardly allows, is certainly not extravagant—$4\frac{1}{2}$. We may meantime adopt it ; but his 4 generations in 215 we cannot adopt in such a calculation. Four lengthened lives of four heads of families he presents to us as the measure of all the generations. The term generation is of the most indefinite kind, signifying long or short, as the case might be ; but here, according to the Bishop's own way, we may assume that the common generations were not much larger than they are in any healthy country. We read (Gen. l. 23), " And Joseph saw Ephraim's children of the third generation : the children also of Machir, the son of Manasseh, were brought upon Joseph's knees." If the fourth generation was reached in Joseph's time, which extended to 70 years of the sojourn in Egypt, according to the common computation, do we take the measure too high at 7 generations in the 215 years of the sojourn ? not counting Kohath the first, as

Colenso, but the one next Kohath. Then the calculation will appear thus :

$$53 \times \overline{5 \cdot 4}^7 = 2{,}019{,}151.$$

We have adopted the number 53 given by the Bishop as all the sons that ever Jacob's sons had, although they were all comparatively young men when they came into Egypt. There is large space here for conjecture.

But the Bishop cannot acquiesce in the ratio he has assumed. He will now bring it down to 3. How does he arrive at this? Not simply by supposing as many daughters as sons; but from observing the numbers given in Ex. vi. He finds they average at 3. But, unfortunately for his ratio, these are "heads of families"—chiefs in Israel (Ex. vi. 14).

Let us look at this matter more attentively.

The Bishop calculates by a very modest ratio, $4\frac{1}{2}$, and by too limited a range of generations—four, *i.e.*, four lengthened lives which, as generations, extend through the 215 years we have agreed to accept as the period of sojourn.

His table of generations may be exhibited thus (Ex. vi. 16—20, 23):

Names.	Sons.	On being in Egypt.	Lived.
Levi	3	0	137
Kohath	4	66	133
Amram	2 & 1 d.	66	137
Aaron	4	60	83 at the Exodus.
Eleazar	—	23	23 at the Exodus.
		215	

The above is evidently not a fair representation of *when* men had children, and of *how many* they had, seeing the length of their lives. We might find examples not a few of four long lives extending through a great period, by having sons late in life—Abraham, Isaac, Jacob, Joseph, extending to 287 years from the calling of Abraham. But during these lives, how many *common* generations might there be? And the ratio adduced is far from extreme. We might invite attention to the passage (Gen. xxii. 20—23); likewise to the record of Esau's genealogy (Gen. xxxvi. 4, with v. 12, if an exception to this be not found in Gen. xiv. 7). Also, during a succeeding period of about 430 years, we might point to the vast increase of Levites in David's time (1 Chron. xxiv., xxv., xxvi. ; and of the other tribes, chap. xxvii). But holding to the account given in Gen. l. 23, that Joseph saw Ephraim's children of the third generation, during 70 years of the sojourn, and likewise to the account of Joshua's descent (1 Chron. vii. 22—27), the seventh from Joseph ; also, observing that the very examples which Dr. Colenso adduces as exceptions furnish examples of even a higher ratio (see 1 Chron. vii. 20 ; viii. 37, 38 ; ix. 43, 44), we may admit generally of the ratio 4.5, but must insist upon the *seven* generations, by which we obtain the number given at the Exodus.

The persistence of Dr. Colenso in his four generations, involves these suppositions :—

1. He must suppose all the lives to have been equally long, and all the men to have their children very late in life ; also that those named were all their children.

2. So thus he must leave out all the collateral branches.

3. He forgets that the men whom he does select as examples, were all heads of families, chiefs, " heads of their fathers' houses " (Ex. vi. 14), the minor branches, as Miriam, not being mentioned.

We have seen how some have laboured much to retain the 430 years, in order to leave room for the multitudinous increase. The Bishop on the other, we have seen, equally strenuous for the 215 years. The numbers, indeed, have been a great stumbling block in the way of commentators, and been the means of exhibiting how men will strain to make out an interpretation. It must have been noticed that some expositors have yielded to the necessity of supposing that inter-marrying with the Egyptians must have prevailed, and that a considerable amount of amalgamation must have obtained. Certainly this is not a very desirable supposition, when we think how pure we should like the line of Israel to have been. Much less, therefore, can we go into the idea that of the "mixed multitude" that went up with the Israelites, not a few might be incorporated with the commonwealth of Israel. Others, again, would try the solution of the difficulty of the number by supposing a mistranscription of the Hebrew *numerals*. But the particularity and minuteness of the numbering of the tribes, as given in Num. xxvi., sets aside all such suppositions. Mistranscriptions have occurred, it is admitted, through the human instrumentality, yet none have been permitted to occur without the means being provided of rectifying them. But this way of dealing wholesale with the numbers, is a kind of handling which the internal structure of the narrative has placed beyond our reach. We may give such interpretations as may be allowed by the nature of the narrative; but where interpretation fails, we must accept of the simple statement upon the general foundation of its being the dictation of the Spirit.

X.—THE DANITES AND LEVITES.

On the same subject of numbers, we have a chapter (xviii.) "on the Danites and Levites at the time of the Exodus."

The author thinks that Dan, with his one son and one family in Israel, might have numbered at the Exodus 27 warriors, instead of 62,700 (Num. ii. 26), or 64,400 (Num. xxvi. 43). He reckons by the ratio of 3 and by 4 generations, making the monstrous supposition in the Scripture account of 80 children of both sexes, to each of Dan's sons and grandsons. This calculation is erroneous, but even the correct one is monstrous.

He cannot here help adverting to the anomaly that the offspring of the one son of Dan, 62,700, is represented as nearly double that of the ten sons of Benjamin, 35,400.

He seems to take especial delight in adverting to the three sons of Levi, reckoning them to the fourth generation at the ratio of 3 at an average, we may estimate.

Finally, he thinks it involves a great inconsistency that during the thirty-eight years in the wilderness, the Levites increased only by 1000. Whereas, supposing that the Levites were exempted from the common punishment of falling in the wilderness, the 22,000 of the first numbering, should have amounted to 48,471 of the second. The tribe of Manasseh, though of the number that fell in the wilderness, from 32,000, amounted to 52,700 men, none of the 32,000 being included.

The Bishop sagely concludes with this remark, "It must now, surely, be sufficiently plain that the account of these numbers is of no statistical value whatever."

Still he cannot have done, but now taking up the rate of increase in England (23 per cent. in 10 years), and reckoning the males at half the population, he finds the 51 males (in Gen. xlvi.), increased in 215 years to 4,375, instead of 1,000,000. So stating, he asks what we are to think of the camping and marching of the Israelites, of their fighting with Amalek and Midian, of the 44 Levites slaying 3000 of the children of Israel, of the children of Israel dying by pestilence, 14,700 at one time, 24,000 at another, as well as of the whole body of 600,000 fighting men, being swept away during the forty years' sojourn in the wilderness? How were the 44 Levites to discharge the work of 8580 (Num. iv. 48)? How were they, with the two priests and their families, to occupy forty-eight cities? How could the tabernacle have been erected out of a levy of silver upon 603,550 men not existing?

I certainly think the Bishop has here said his worst. The tone might have been consonant to an enemy. The spirit that dictated those reflections should be seriously sifted.

At a ratio somewhat higher than he makes it, and in seven generations, it will be nothing incredible to find the family of Dan increased to the number stated.

The apparent anomaly of 62,700 arising from the one son of Dan, and of only 35,400 from the ten sons of Benjamin, is one of those phases in divine providence which may be discerned, but cannot be accounted for.

The reckoning of the three sons of Levi, at the ratio of three, to the fourth generation has been shown to be false. The heads of families only are given : if we are to reckon, we are to take a *reasonable* ratio, and to *seven* generations.

The increase of the Levites from 22,000 to 23,000 during the sojourn in the wilderness, is certainly not great. But this would appear to be incredible, indeed, if, as the Bishop thinks, they were not subjected to the common punishment of falling in the wilderness to the extent of all that rebelled, *i.e.*, that came out of Egypt. The contrary, however, appears to be obvious.

This is the opinion of Scott, and with good reason, if we consider Num. xxvi. 62—65. The Bishop of Clogher thinks also, that not only did the Levites execute judgment in the instance of the golden calf, but that they executed judgment principally on their own tribe. (Ex. xxxii. 28, 35; Deut. xxxiii. 9)—Chron. of the Heb. Bib. p. 360.

The contrast drawn between them and the tribe of Manasseh, is then not so striking.

When the Bishop takes up the rate of increase of population in England, we should suppose he would be at home. He now measures what might be the increase of the Hebrews in 215 years, by the increase common in England. Here it might not be presumpuous to advise the study of our standard writers on Political Economy. The difference of increase in a new colony and in an old country is great and obvious. In an old and thickly peopled country like England, three causes powerfully operate to retard the progress of population. As soon as a people reaches the extent of its country's supplies, they find an insuperable obstacle to increase. Again, in the present condition of mankind, all thickly peopled countries are filled with vice, which shortens human existence. Once more, and more than all, marriage is prevented or retarded to a large degree in such countries, and so correspondingly the progress of population. To these three causes, which have been pointed out at large in works on national economy, I may add a fourth, which, for upwards of 200 years has been operating sensibly in this country, in diminishing the increase of population. Since the discovery of America, the tide of emigration has been flowing on. Still more so, since the design to overtake the fields of Australia, and other places, began. We find ourselves very much like the populous states of ancient Greece, which sent off her redundant population to the Chersonesus. The mighty Rome disposed of her own swarming armies, by disposing them among the conquered provinces. Even before the time of our Saviour, the Jews had spread themselves through the rich regions of Asia-Minor, unknowingly preparing the way for the wide reach of the Gospel. Spain in the height of her prosperity could spare multitudes for her new-found regions in North and

South America. So Britain has been long sending to hers, and for this, and the other causes mentioned above, hindrances to marriage, poverty and the vice of intemperance, above all, she cannot be made a comparison, in point of increase in population to a young and rising nation, even in Egypt or afterwards in Canaan. . The Bishop should read Sumner, the late Archbishop of his own church, on this subject. It is laid down that the rate of advance in a new people, with a new country, is, that it doubles its population in about every 15 years. Let us try the Hebrew people at this acknowledged ratio. The result is as follows:—

$$53 \times 2^{14} = 1,736,704.$$

Looking over the rise and progress of some of the States of America, which used to be called the new world, I was struck with the account of Pensylvania. In commencement, in extent of teritory, whether in reference to Egypt or Canaan, in progress of population in about the same period, the comparison between the people of Pensylvania and the Hebrews holds wonderfully. Immigration has swelled Pensylvania to some extent: we cannot say that the Hebrews received no acquisition particularly on the female side. With all this, the two are very similar.

The Bishop's concluding paragraph on this chapter is remarkable. I would not that I had given it to world in print. I would have asked, May I not have mistaken in my calculation? He sneers throughout. Camping and marching! 44 Levites slaying 3,000 of the children of Israel! Dying of pestilence in thousands! Half-a-million swept off in the wilderness! 44 Levites doing the work of 8,580! 48 Cities to them, and two priests and their families! The Tabernacle erected out of contributions from 603,550 warriors who did not exist! The Bishop has said his worst.

XI.—THE TWO NUMBERINGS (Ex. xxxviii. 24—26, and Num. i. 46).

On the numbering of the people, (Num. 1.) as compared with the poll-tax (Ex. xxxviii. 1.) the Bishop cannot avoid insinuating.

He asks, "How could they be taxed after the shekel of the sanctuary, when no sanctuary existed?" "Shekel of the sanctuary"—possibly so named, says Scott, because the standard weight was kept there. But the Bishop says, no sanctuary yet existed. Suppose a historian, at some subsequent time when a certain value of money had come to be called by a specific name, having occasion to refer to that value, he would likely use that name in speaking of a prior money transaction. This is all.

The Bishop quotes the command, (Ex. xxx. 11—13) that when Israel should be numbered, each man should pay in ransom for his soul half a shekel. He says that in Ex. xxxviii. 26, he reads of such a tribute being paid, and that in Num. i. (6 months after, he says) he reads of the numbering being made. "He suggests that, in the former place, the numbering may be omitted, and, in the latter, the half shekel," his object being to show there were two distinct numberings. And then he says, "It is surprising that the number of adult males should have been identically the same (603,550) on the first occasion as it was half a year afterwards."

It certainly appears, that the two events, though virtually one, give the number of Israel at two different periods, however short the time. Ithamar is appointed to take note of the things given for the service of the sanctuary, while Moses and Aaron superintend the numbering of the people. There is the command (Ex. xxx.) to tax when they numbered. Necessarily the tax is required (Ex. xxxviii.) for the erection of the Tabernacle, while sometime afterwards the number of the people is taken (Num. 1). The two things should have been simultaneously, according to Ex. xxx., and in this sense they are one. But whereas they occurred at two different times, they are in this sense two. The question then is, how comes it to pass that the sum is the same at both times. The Bishop insists, that these are two distinct numberings at the different times, the one by the half shekel, the other by the individual.*

The explanation of Kurtz, that both places have reference to one event, that in Exodus to the ransom, and that in Numbers

---

* The opinion of Michallis and Havanick, which the Bishop quotes and replies to, are entitled to respect.

to the census; and that as the difference in point of numbers would be very small in the short time, the result of the numbering might be employed in ascertaining the amount of the poll tax. The Bishop will not admit of this, and he has reason, for we find Ithamar appointed expressly to take note of the offerings. To cover any difference that might have arisen in the numbers in the course of the time, Kurtz further points to the integral hundreds in the summation of the tribes. Hereupon the Bishop points to the odd 50 in the tribe of Gad; and when he finds Kurtz next explaining that the Israelites may have been numbered in *fifties*, meets the explanation with the statement, that at the second numbering (Num. xxvi.), there is, in the tribe of Reuben, an odd number of 30, which he will not allow to have been a mistranscription, but which, he insists, shows that the individual numbers were taken. The notion of a special providence in there numbers, which one commentator piously suggests, the Bishop will not admit, as such is not mentioned in the narative, and I cannot find any call to admit such on this occasion. The Bishop is refractory on any concessions to conjecture; he will adhere to the historic account, which must be able to bear out itself, to all men's satisfaction, whatever may be their means of judging. I cannot but think he has in this department of historical investigation, opened up a field that will employ him to the full contentment of his peculiar talent, through a long life. But in a short time, I conjecture he will have all the pleasure to himself; for very few will go through the drudgery and waste of precious time, in following him in Episcopal impertinence.

The Bishop will allow of no mistake in the count. Moses and Aaron must not deal as did Joab, when David sent him to number the people (2 Sam. xxiv.)—they must not assume. Ithamar must be exact to a gerah. In fact, to satisfy the Bishop, he and you would have required to stand by the scales; and then he might have questioned the sight of his own eyes. Had he ever stood in a moulder's, and seen how rapidly the admeasurements of one set of things went on; or in a potter's, and witnessed the manufacture; or even in the more accurate mint, and witnessed coin-making, he would have received a salutary lesson.

Now, the matter here is not so prodigious as the Bishop would represent it. Look here, he seems to say, at this extraordinary account. He will cling to the exact numbers—the very 50—he will not omit a single individual. He will have it, that these are exactly the things that the historian states, which is so singular that it bears upon the face of it imposture. Well, let us look; what do we see? To a simple-minded reader, the two places (Ex. xxxviii. and Num. i.) refer to one event—the former to the ransom, the latter to the polling; but the ransom anticipates the polling (see Ex. xxx. 11—16), for this reason, that the Tabernacle required to be immediately erected. To the Bishop we would say, the sum of Israel is given in Exodus according to the half shekel, but nothing of the tribes. In the interval between this and the regular numbering, variations would occur in all the tribes by diminution and augmentation, by deaths and births; and what prodigious is there if, at the end of a few months, the number of Israel turns out to be the same? Still more wonderful, the sum of Israel at the end of the 38 years is found to be nearly the same (Num. xxvi. 51), so equally had the numbers of increase and decrease kept. As to the numbering mentioned in Num. i., considerable increase may be conceived to have taken place, although the number appears to be the same, if we allow, as I think we must, that the old and unserviceable, who must all have been counted under the assessment, as every man had to give a ranson for his soul, were not included in this regular numbering for war (Num. i. 3); and if, also, we take this into account, that the Levites, who, it would seem, had to pay the ransom also, not then being named for the Lord, were not numbered here among the men fit for war (Num. i. 47—49).

XII.—THE FIRST-BORN.

The design in chapter xiv. of the Bishop's book is to show that the number of the First-born bears no adequate proportion to the number of the people. The number is 22,273, which implies the prodigious average of 42 male children in every family. Kurtz and other previous commentators have received the same idea of the first-born that Colenso assumes, which will be stated immediately, and hence the great labour it has cost them to give a feasible account of the matter. I do not go into their arguments, being convinced that the same proportions hold through all the members of the family, whether we refer to births or deaths, or even deaths under the cruel order of Pharoah. The "first-born," according to the Bishop, comprehended all that were first-born, whatever was their age and their standing, whether the families of which they were the first-born were existing or extinct. Learned men differ as to who were the first-born in remote antiquity; some holding it was the head of the family or community, as Abraham and Melchisedec; others, that the eldest son was instituted the high priest of the family. Bishop Clayton inclines to adopt the former opinion, and, confining the title of first-born to the father, grandfather, or great-grandfather, as the constituted priest of the family, argues that the calculations concerning the number of the first-born will not be so unreasonable (p. 363). This opinion of Bishop Clayton, though plasuible, I cannot entertain in the face of Scripture representation of the first-born. The latter opinion, of the first-born sons being by birth the priests of the Lord, " seems," says Scott, "to have no Scriptural ground. The Levites, as substituted for the first-born, were not admitted to the priesthood; nor were they exchanged for the first-born of mature age, but for the young first-born children." We do find something in ancient poetry and history, if I recollect aright, of sons of kings being constituted priests; but it is with the Scripture idea of the first-born that we have at present to do. Bishop Colenso takes the widest range, the father of the family, if first-born, also his first-born son, and this son's first-born. You see what he will arrive at—that the number stated of 22,273 first-born, in comparison of 2,000,000 of people, is utterly incompatible. He wants, beyond this, to prove that the 2,000,000 did not exist save in the "unhistorical" narrative. On this department of the argument, Bishop Colenso lays great weight, exposing his conscious weakness, however, in others, by the unlucky expression (p. 117), "We have shown that the number of years, according to the story, was 215, instead of 430, and the number of generations *four*, instead of fourteen. But, independently of these, there remains the difficulty of Levi's descendants, and of the number of the first-born." Let us, then, as a fundamental point, ascertain what is the Scripture idea of the first-born.

There cannot be a doubt that the " firstlings " among cattle that were to be offered, were the young and not the old ; so are we to understand by the " first-born" among men. In Isaac's family the point is clearly exhibited again and again—the first-born of the family. As in cattle, so we might say here, it was not the old and infirm that the Lord chose for his active service, but the young, the " beginning of strength." According to Bishop Colenso, while Isaac lived there were four first-borns in one line, Isaac himself, who was inheritor; Jacob, who was first-born and heir by contract; Reuben, who was Jacob's first-born ; and Hanoch, who was Reuben's. The Bishop will have it that the "first-born" means the oldest, though the family of which he is first-born be extinct, and he himself have become the head of a family. Would any one understand it was the father or oldest in the family that lay dead on that terrible night when the Lord smote all the first-born in the land of Egypt ? So when the Lord said, " Sanctify unto me all the first-born, whatsoever openeth the womb among the children of Israel, of man and of beast : it is mine," would not each father understand it to mean the beginning of his strength, the first of his family, and not himself, if he had been a first-born ? It is always the first-born of *existing* families ; and though the father of the family may have been a first-born himself, he is no longer named as such when he comes to have a family himself. The first-born child IS the "first-born," and if the first-born be a male, he is of the "first-born " signified in the Scripture history. But the Bishop will have it that what is meant by the first-born is the oldest; and not only so, but the oldest in every stage downward, from great-grandfather, grandfather, and father. Now, all along the Scripture account is, that it is the oldest child of the existing family. There is a remarkable passage to this effect in Deut. xxi. 15—17 : " If a man have two wives, one beloved and another hated, and they have born him children, both the beloved and the hated ; and if the first-born son be her's that is hated; then it shall be, when he maketh his sons to inherit that which he hath, that he may not make the son of the beloved first-born before the son of the hated, which is indeed the first-born : but he shall acknowledge the son of the hated for the first-born, by giving him a double portion of all that he hath ; for he is the beginning of his strength ; the right of the first-born is his."

And not even the first-born of familes as they existed in coming out of Egypt are the particular first-born meant, though the reason assigned for choosing the first-born might seem to have pre-eminent reference to *them*, being spared amid the common slaughter, we might say, that they might be devoted to the Lord. The command to set apart all the first-born had reference to the *future*—from that time forward. Ex. xiii. 11, " And it shall be, when the Lord shall bring thee into the land of the Canaanites, as he sware unto thee and to thy fathers, and shall give it thee, that thou shalt set apart unto the Lord all that openeth the matrix, and every firstling that cometh of a beast which thou hast ; the males shall be the Lord's." Then when the transference is made to the tribe of Levi, in place of the first-born, it is said (Num. iii. 40), " And the Lord said unto Moses, Number all the first-born of the males of the children of Israel, from a month old and upward, and take the number of their names." Here are the first-born from the time the command was given (Ex. xiii). Colenso, however, will not yield this point. He argues that the description "from a month old and upward," being applied to the Levites without limitation as to age, applies also to the first-born without limitation (p. 89). Suppose the command had been, Number all the males in the tribe of Levi, from a month old and upward, and all the first-born infant males of the tribes of Israel, it would be seen at once that there was limitation in the latter which was not in the former. Now, the proper definition of "first-born" marks this very limitation.

I shall close this argument by adverting to a comparison between the number of the first-born and that of the Levites, which might seem at first to militate against me. We find the number of the Levites to be 22,300 (Num. iii. 22, 28, 34). Now, there must be a reason for the number of Levites being said to be only 22,000 (v. 39), and what can that reason be, but that the 300 of difference had already been struck off as first-born to the Lord ? So there remained 22,000 Levites, to redeem or stand for 22,000 first-born sons. And as for the 273 first-born that were over and above the number of the Levites, five shekels were appointed to be given for their ransom-price. On the very face, therefore, of this whole transaction we read, that the first-born were limited in range, and confined to the eldest child in each family, from the period at which the command was given to sanctify unto the Lord all the first-born, whatever openeth the womb among the children of Israel (Ex. xiii. 2).

This brings the question to an issue. The probable number of births of such a multitude in one year we may approximate, calculating according to the ratio of a fresh colony; and as to the first-borns, from the time specified, and in the circumstances, the number stated, 22,273, seems to be a fair increase. Most satisfaction, I think, will be found in the explanation which Scott has given, which Colenso does not meet otherwise than in the way of querulousness (Scott's Commentary; Notes on Num. iii. 41—43).

The sacred historian states these particulars with seriousness and sobriety. I would here ask Bishop Colenso, were he present, what motive any historian could have in fabricating "stories." He must suppose, that some have contrived to present the whole that Moses wrote in the highest style of exaggeration. He will not say, Moses himself so gave the history forth. Then what a mighty labour must all this have involved, and what an imposition to be palmed upon a nation! The Bishop has taken up a railing accusation, failing to see, all the time, the position which he himself holds in reference to the professed beliefs of the Church of England. Look here, Colenso, at this Right Reverend Prelate of Natal, sent out to translate the Books of Moses as part of the oracles of Jehovah, and to proclaim to sinners the Saviour therein typified, with mind darkened and perverted, subverting the faith which he was sent to propagate. The prelates of England, I hope, will speak out, and if there be grace and the spirit of submission within him, will convince the man, already in the wake of a renegade. If, unhappily, otherwise, they will see to it that one in the guise of their own order shall not, as a virtual enemy, occupy one of the citadels of the common faith.

XIII.—AT THE DOOR OF THE TABERNACLE.

IN some of his chapters, we may relax our attention as the Bishop is evidently indulging himself. Here is one (iv.): he is in the vein of admeasurement. We cannot help admiring his *twenty miles*. Seriously, he was not much taken up with his proper work—the souls of men in the province of Natal.

His subject is this: "And the Lord spake unto Moses, saying . . . . Gather thou all the congregation together unto the door of the Tabernacle of the congregation. And Moses did as the Lord commanded him; and the assembly was gathered together unto the door of the Tabernacle of the congregation" (Lev. viii. 1, 3, 4).

He quotes several passages to show that the words rendered Assembly and Congregation convey more in the above quotation, than that the elders only were assembled at the door of the Tabernacle; that they convey, that the whole body of the people are to be understood. We do not feel disposed to deny that he is right, though on such occasions the "elders" are often the parties named (Ex. xii. 21, xxiv. 1; Lev. ix. 1). The words run: "And gather thou all the congregation together unto the door of the tabernacle of assembling. And Moses did as the Lord commanded him; and the congregation was gathered together unto the door of the tabernacle of assembling. The word conveys the sense of its being the whole people without limitation. The Bishop, however, will be content with the 603,550 men (Num. ii. 32). Let him have his own way in this. He is now going to show an enormous thing. "As the text says distinctly 'at the door of the tabernacle,' they must have come *within the court*. And this, indeed, was necessary for the purpose for which they were summoned on this occasion, namely, to witness the ceremony of the consecration of Aaron and his sons to the priestly office. This was to be performed inside the tabernacle itself, and could only, therefore, be seen by those standing at the door."

The Bishop now draws his wondrous conclusions. Having shown us the breadth of the tabernacle, before which all the congregation was to stand, in the presence of the Lord, he makes it clear that, if they all stand in front, nine in a line with due space between the lines, the multitude will extend back twenty miles. Then, further, he gives us the admeasurement of the court—a length of 100 cubits, by 50 in breadth—showing that if the multitude now occupy the breadth of the court, in place of being all within it, they will now stretch back four miles. This would be neither *at the door* of the Tabernacle, nor *within the court* of the Tabernacle, nor would the greater part of the people be even within seeing, and what an enormous statement is it, that "the Assembly was gathered unto the door of the Tabernacle of the Congregation."

A plain man reading the passage would make no difficulty of the matter at all. He would think, if he thought on this particular at all, they all assembled as near the door as they could. The Bishop is addressing a congregation, and he writes home that he had 1000 natives before him, hearing the word. We follow the Bishop's plan, we measure, and finding that, with nine in front, the congregation extends one-third of a mile, we say, what an egregious blunder!

The Bishop is inexorable. Because he cannot compress the mighty bulk within the limited space of the court, which perhaps might not be extended, he leaves the inference as to the historian's veracity to be adduced.

How forcible is an AT—*at the door* of the tabernacle of the congregation. But if they could not all, they could not. First come, first there, at the door; the rest as near as they might attain. Plainly, however, it does not appear "that the consecration took place *within* the tabernacle at all, but rather *at the door of it* (see Lev. ix. 23), so that Aaron would be within sight; and the command is not, to gather the people *at* the door, but *to* the door, facing the door as much as might be, and as near as possible—there being nothing said about being within the court or without it. This is all. The witnessing of the consecration of the High Priest, Type of Christ, is the great thing intended.

XIV.—THE LAW READ IN THE HEARING OF ALL ISRAEL.

BISHOP COLENSO desires it to be understood, that by one man, Moses, and afterwards Joshua, the Law was read in the hearing of all Israel, at one time. We have had reason, on several occasions, to examine the Bishop's quotations by parallel passages, to ascertain the correctness of his expositions. In the present instance we are not satisfied, that Moses personally read all the Law, in the hearing of all the people, at one time. In the course of his remarks, the Bishop confines himself to Joshua; but, prefacing this chapter with the words, "Moses and Joshua addressing all Israel," he leaves it to be concluded, that Moses, as well as Joshua, addressed all Israel, in all the Law, in one day. His quotations from Deu. i. 1, and v. 1, confirm this supposition. We read, "These be the words which Moses spake unto all Isrrel, on this side Jordan, in the wilderness, in the plain over against the Red Sea (rather Zuph) between Paran, and Tophel, and Laban, and Hazeroth, and Dizahab." The very reading of these words would suggest different times and different places. Then, in Deu. xxvii. 1, we read, "And Moses, with the Elders of Israel, commanded the people, saying, Keep all the commandments which I command you this day." The Elders of Israel are here associated with him in charging the people. At the 9th verse we read, "And Moses, and the priests the Levites, spake unto all Israel, saying, Take heed and hearken, O Israel; this day thou art become the people of the Lord thy God." The singular pronoun, "I," occurs as the regular form, yet from these quotations, it appears that others were associated with him in delivering the words, "Keep all the commandments which I command you this day." Whence it appears, that, if all the Law was charged upon all the people, it was done by one, as chief, having many assistants; and, in respect of the terms "this day," they are of the most indefinite import. Then, further, as to the special duty to be performed by Joshua, when he should have led the people into the promised land, we read here also that the Levites take large part (verse 14), "And the Levites shall speak, and say unto all the men of Israel with a loud voice." So we would be warranted in interpreting the quotation of Bishop Colenso from Joshua viii. 34, 35, "And afterwards he read all the words of the Law, the blessings and the cursings, according to all that is written in the book of the Law. There was not a word of all that Moses commanded, which Joshua read not before all the congregation of Israel, with the women, and the little ones, and the strangers, that were conversant among them."

But the Bishop insists that the history gives out that all the Law was read by one man, Joshua, in one day, in the hearing of all Israel. Thereupon he asks, in effect, how it was possible that Joshua should read all that was commanded, where no human voice, unless strengthened by a miracle, of which Scripture tells us nothing, could have reached the hearing of a mass of people as large as the whole population of London. He will not allow that the Law may have been read, first to one body of the people, then to another, and so on, till the whole had heard it, for he says, "The day would not have sufficed for reading in this way all the blessings and the cursings; much less, all the words of the Law, many times over, especially after that he (Joshua) had been already engaged, as the story implies, on the very same day, in writing a copy of the Law of Moses upon the stones set up in Mount Ebal." And he will not admit that Joshua, first himself, and then by delegation, or simultaneously by delegation, read all the Law, and the Blessings and the Cursings, in the hearing of the people—he will have it to be said, that it was all done by Joshua alone, even though Deut. xxvii. 9—14, says otherwise as to the Exhortations, and specially as to the Blessings and the Cursings which the Levites pronounced with a loud voice. We shall, therefore, indulge the Bishop in his vein.

Joshua, having penetrated into the heart of the land, takes heed to obey the command (Deut. xxvii.) as to the words of the Law, and as to the uttering of the Blessings and the Cursings. The space between Mount Gerizim and Mount Ebal is the appointed place. Commencing at the middle of the vale, and thence ascending a mile on each side, and extending lengthwise three quarters of a mile, you have the whole space required for the assembled people. There conceive all to be assembled that were able, and that Joshua reads in the Law, and the people hear, as far as human voice can extend. This would be really obedience to the command. Now sound would go very far in such a place. Confined on each side, the voice of one speaking above would be very distinctly heard by multitudes in the valley below. Many of us have experienced this in our tours in the Highlands. Dr. Buchanan, in his "Clerical Furlough," adduces a striking instance of this—two shepherds talking to each other across the valley of the Kedron, where it would have taken a full hour to pass from one to the other (Cl. F., p. 257). The people fill up the mighty space. All eyes are turned towards one direction as much as might be; and in the calmness of such a valley, and under what we might conceive a serene sky, the Leader of Israel reads the Law, and the Levites utter the blessings and the cursings, and on each being uttered, all the people say, Amen.

This is the ceremonial of the day. The mere reading of the Law was not all that was intended. Besides, those that heard could not from the single reading retain. Whence the Law was required to be impressed on plaistered stones, to be set up on Mount Ebal, and seen and read by all the people (Deu. xxvii. 4, 8; Josh. viii. 32).

And already all Israel had now heard all the commandments of Jehovah many times, during the thirty-eight years of wandering in the wilderness. Possibly they had large transcriptions of it. And they were to be afterwards fully taught in the Statutes of the Lord (Deu. xxvii. 14; 2 Chron. xxxv. 3; Neh. viii. 7).

But the public act was important. The thousands of Israel assembled by divine command, the tablets containing Jehovah's laws produced, Joshua in a conspicious place, prepared to read, the presence of Jehovah would be felt, and the vast multitude awed into reverence.

Bishop Colenso can take in nothing of this.

XV.—EXTENT OF CANAAN.

The Bishop quotes Ex. xxiii. 27-30 : the point taken up being, " I will not drive them (the inhabitants) out from before thee in one year, lest the land become desolate, and the beasts of the field multiply against thee."

He measures that part of the promised land which was divided among the tribes in Joshua's time—giving us the amount of miles and acres—and finds that it would have been as thickly populated as three of the great counties of England at the present day, Norfolk, Suffolk, Essex, even without reckoning the aboriginal Canaanites, who already filled the land—seven nations, greater and mightier than Israel. We have come to feel when reading any very simple statements of the Bishop, that we are treading upon treacherous ground. Having made a comparison between the portion of Canaan in view and these three counties of England, he observes, " And surely it cannot be said that these three Eastern Counties, with their flourishing towns (which he names, not seeing that the towns would draw in the more from the country), are in any danger of lying 'desolate,' with the beasts of the field multiplying against the human inhabitants." This is an observation of pure innocence and simplicity.

He adduces, for a comparison, the colony of Natal, which being one and a half times the size of Canaan, and requiring a population as 3 to 2 to be equally filled, is in no danger of being overrun with wild beasts with a population not the twelfth part of that which is said to have entered the land of Canaan. Innocent still!

The Bishop is an adept in Physical Geography; competent to give an opinion on cattle and acres, desert land and wild beasts. Simple as the conclusions are which he draws above, they are insidious in the extreme. The implication is, the Scripture account agrees not with what must have been the actual state of things : whence so great a multitude of people did not enter Canaan.

There is a fallacious mode of reasoning, of which our mental philosophy writers used to complain—that of reasoning under a term of different significations. You will find the fallacy of the

Bishop's statements here in the single expression—"The whole land, which was divided among the tribes in the time of Joshua, including the countries beyond the Jordan, was, in extent, about 11,000 square miles, or 7,000,000 acres." Now, was this all that was meant by "Canaan"? Was this all that they were promised? The name Canaan, as used by Bishop Colenso in chapter xiii., on the extent of Canaan, is most ambigious, denoting a part of the land, and then the whole land. That the whole land was not possessed by the Israelites in the time of Joshua is plain, from passages which I shall immediately quote. Passages showing as if the Israelites had obtained possession of the whole in Joshua's days, are such as these—Josh. xi. 23, xix. 49, xxi. 43-45. Passages showing that they were not to obtain all at once, are such as these—Ex. xxxiii. 29-31; Deu. xi. 22-25. Passages showing that they did not obtain possession of all the land during the days of Joshua, are these—Josh. xiii. 6, and xviii. 10, compared with xxiii. 4, 5, 13. And the following are instances —xiii. 6, xv. 63, xvi. 10, xvii. 12, 18; Judges i. 17-21. I repeat, Does the Bishop's statement above-given comprehend all that the Israelites were promised—the wide dominions to which Solomon attained? (1 Kings iv. 21) "And Solomon reigned over all (the) kingdoms, from the river (Euphrates) unto the land of the Philistines, and unto the border of Egypt." Even though the people of Israel did not extend so widely as the dominion of Solomon, I suppose it is thoroughly consistent with the true state of things to say, that had all the "seven nations" been at once driven out, the land would largely have become desolate, and the beast of the field would have multiplied against them.

XVI.—EXTENT OF THE CAMP.

THE Bishop keeps up the subject of Size with evident satisfaction, and now with reference to the duties of the priest. He sets to work like a master-builder, to give the exact dimensions of the Camp (chap. vi.), supposing the Camp to be a mile and a half across in each direction. His design is obvious, which is to show the impossibility of the Priest performing certain of his functions. It is written (Lev. iv. 11, 12), "And the skin of the bullock, and all his flesh, with his head, and with his legs and his inwards, and his dung, even the whole bullock, shall he [the Priest] carry forth without the Camp, unto a clean place, where the ashes are poured out, and burn him on the wood with fire. Where the ashes are poured out, there shall he be burned." These parts of the bullock are to be carried out by the Priest himself (Aaron, or one of his two sons, Eleazar or Ithamar) a distance of three-quarters of a mile. He says, also, the refuse of these sacrifices specified in the passage would have to be carried out by the Priest himself, Aaron, or Eleazar, or Ithamar.

Even yet he thinks he has not stated enough. Forthwith, as frequently, he goes into another element of objection, and says that from the outside of this great Camp wood and water would have to be brought for all purposes, if such supplies as these could be obtained at all. Then the ashes of the whole Camp, with the rubbish and filth of every kind of this vast multitude, would have to be carried out amid the crowded mass of people.

Having quoted an obnoxious passage from Deuteronomy, for the purpose of extending the difficulty, he next presents the foregoing objections under the aspect of a Camp extended now to the size of twelve miles square, so that the aged Aaron, or one of his sons, will have to carry the burden a distance of six miles.

These are the objections presented in this chapter. They will not greatly alarm the most sensitive believer. The priest is appointed to carry forth the burden (Lev. iv. 12). We shall allow that the Hiphil form of a neuter verb has only the effect generally of rendering the verb active. So, in the present instance, *yatza*, to go out, being in the Hiphil form, *hotzi*, literally, he shall cause to go out, the signification simply is, he shall take forth, or carry forth, or shall have forth without the Camp. Thus much for the verbal import, and with this the natural import must be taken. Even apart from any help to the interpretation derived from the history, common sense would tell us that if the work involved an impossibility, the priest must get help to do it. And, certainly, this kind of work might as well be done by another. It was not like the scape-goat carrying away guilt; it was one carrying away refuse. But the right answer from the history is at hand: the Levites were given to Aaron that they might assist in many of the duties. We read (Num. viii. 18, 19), "And I have taken the Levites for all the first-born of the children of Israel. And I have given the Levites as a gift to Aaron, and to his sons, from among the children of Israel, to do the service of the children of Israel in the tabernacle of the congregation, and to make an atonement [to make atonement] for the children of Israel; that there be no plague among the children of Israel, when the children of Israel come nigh unto the sanctuary." In our next article—the Duties of the Priests—we shall more particularly distinguish between the duties which were peculiar to the priests, and those wherein the Levites might bear part with them. We shall also have occasion, when we come to consider the Passover, to refer to instances wherein the Levites of necessity performed the most sacred service, both for the people and for the priests. Certainly there was no particular sacredness about the mere carrying out of the bullock, though there was significance in the intent of burning him without the Camp; and as to the assistants, this might appear appropriate work. Commonly among men, the command given to a superior, and the fulfilment of it on his part, very frequently embraces the service of an inferior. The Queen and her Government are said to do what is done by a thousand agents.*

* While I am preparing this article on the Camp for the press, the Bishop's Second Book. or Part II. on the Pentateuch and the Book of Joshua, is put into my hand. I am directed to a long list of Corrections and Additions to be made in Part I., first edition. Of this I shall take special notice in my Notes at the end. Meantime, as to the article on the Camp, I find sundry corrections and additions. On the priest's obligation to carry forth the bullock himself out of the Camp, I am directed to insert after Lev. iv. 11, 12, the following—" And the priest shall put on his linen garment, and his linen breeches shall he put upon his flesh, and take up the ashes which the fire hath consumed with the burnt-offering on the altar, and he shall put them beside the altar. And he shall put off his garments, and put on other garments, and carry forth the ashes without the camp unto a clean place" (Lev. vi. 10, 11). Then he inserts, It would rather seem, from the second of the passages above quoted, that *the Priest himself in person* was to do this, and that there is here no room for the application of the principle, *qui facit per aluim, facit per se*. These are the Bishop's additional notes.

As to the refuse of all kinds, "the ashes of the whole Camp, with the rubbish and filth of every kind," the Bishop does not mean to say, that this was to be carried out by the Priest, though he places the work in close proximity to his duties. But if all such prodigious work as he calls up had to be done, it might be done easily by the multitude of strong healthy men. He asks, as frequently, whence the wood and water could be procured that would be certainly required. True enough; but what has all this to do with the priest's duties, the subject of this chapter? I am sorry to see he cannot let slip an occasion of multiplying difficulties against the authenticity of the narrative, though it destroy the unity of his argument. Evidently he is no logician. This department of objection falls under the head of provision for the wilderness (see art. VIII. on chap. xii.) One hint here: for all the Bishop's difficulties, in obtaining supplies when not miraculously afforded, he will find a sufficient supply of physical strength and energy in the 600,000 able men, unless he persist in averring that they had no existence (p. 112).

I am tempted from the expression (p. 39) "and, therefore, must be understood to apply only to the males, or rather only

Some will think how unlucky he is in his quotations, for here is another instransitive verb (*rum*, to be high) presented in the transitive form (*herim*, to lift up, or, as they may say, cause to rise). Likewise, the very reason that he seems to have considered a reason for the work being done by the priest, is indeed a reason for its being capable of being done by any one, viz., the putting off of his sacerdotal robes, and putting on common clothes. Having advanced this additional text in proof of his interpretation, that the priest himself carried all forth, immediately he makes a fatal admission, showing the truth of the adage, *quem Deus vult perdere prius dementat*. He writes, Page 40, line 13, *for* on his back on foot, *read* perhaps with the help of others. The whole argument is here given up, showing after all that this Bishop is reducible to reason. As a further means of bringing him to this proper way of thinking, I would suggest the reading of Lev. xvi. 27, 28. This passage will afford the proper liberal interpretation of the ones quoted above. Some one carries forth the residue of the bullock; some persons burn the residue; then the one that burns it washes himself and his clothes, that he may return to the camp. The passage is this, "And the bullock for the sin-offering, and the goat for the sin-offering, whose blood was brought in to make atonement in the holy place, shall *one* carry forth without the camp; and they shall burn in the fire their skins, and their flesh, and their dung. And he that burneth them shall wash his clothes, and bathe his flesh in water, and afterward he shall come into the camp."

to the 600,000 warriors," to think that the Bishop saw the direct application of the command in Deut. xxiii. 12—14; yet he perversely makes it apply to the whole multitude in the wilderness, and takes occasion to say, it is so limited in its application that it is convincing proof of the unhistorical character of the narrative. In one word, the command applies to the army, compact compared with the mass in the wilderness, with which the Lord was to go out at all times against their enemies.

The Large Camp. The Bishop is fond of pictures. Ministers do sometimes betake themselves to strange trades and strange pursuits. While the Bishop delights in admeasurements, he can try his hand at a picture. His, however, is grotesque in the extreme. The aged Aaron, bending under the weight of the bullock, walks through the tents of Israel, a distance of six miles; and not contented with this, the Bishop presents it under the guise of one going from St. Paul's to the outskirts of the metropolis, exposed, shall we say, to the gaze of the London populace.

XVII.—DUTIES OF THE PRIESTS.

BISHOP COLENSO (chap. xx.) specifies a number of duties to be performed by the Priests: the sprinkling of blood in every burnt-offering, the offering for a woman after childbirth, the cleansing of leprosy, cleanings of various pollutions, the law of separation, the daily lamb, morning and evening, festivals in the seventh month. He insists that all these had to be fulfilled in the wilderness while there were but three Priests. Also he assigns as reason, that the Priests must perform these duties personally (Num. iii. 10), "And thou shalt appoint Aaron and his sons, and they shall wait on their Priest's office; and the stranger that cometh nigh shall be put to death. (See v. 38).

He then particularly specifies one duty, the double sacrifice for women after childbirth, and calculates the amount of duty at the rate of 250 births a-day, which would be 500 sacrifices.

According to custom, he starts away from the immediate subject, and demands where, in the case of women not able to offer a lamb, "turtle doves," or "young pigeons," could be found, in such multitudes, in the wilderness. Following on this, he would know how the vast quantity of meat, of oil, and wine, and wheat, and fruit, could be consumed by so few as the Priests and their families, and all in the most holy place. Nor do his objections end here; he wishes to know how the small number of Priests and their families could occupy thirteen cities set apart for them in the days of Joshua. These exhaust the present chapter.

The Bishop is strenuous on the point, that all the duties he assigns were to be performed in the wilderness, and by the three in the sacerdotal office. And what does he adduce as his great reason for insisting, that they had all to be performed in the wilderness? The occurrence of the word CAMP in connection with the offering of the bullock for the Priest, the offering of the burnt-offering, and the cure of leprosy. The Camp is mentioned again and again; but we have to remember that the whole ritual was intended for Canaan; that it was not the Lord's approved way that the Israelites should wander about in the wilderness at all, but go straightway to the land of promise. The ritual of old, as every code of laws is intended to be, was perfect at the beginning, and intended for a people advancing to the state of a perfect nation of Jehovah. The ritual would be most perfect, being of Jehovah; the people, only advancing in the line of spiritual training, would be imperfect in observance. In the wilderness, therefore, at the beginning of their sacred economy, much would be that would require improvement, and filling up; and certainly if many of these observances depended on the number of Priests, much would necessarily for long remain undone, or be done by means of assistance. But Bishop Colenso holds to the literal interpretation, that all the duties said to be appointed to the Priests must be done by the Priests personally. Then we ask for what were the Levites given? We have already quoted to show that the Levites were to assist in the most sacred duties, though not in all the duties (Num. viii. 19). I quote from Jennings on the Jewish Antiquities, (p. 139); "The first class (of Levites in David's time) were to wait upon the sons of Aaron, for the service of the house of the Lord; that is, to assist the priests in the exercise of their ministry, to purify the holy things, to prepare the shew bread, and flour, and wine, and oil for the sacrifice; and sometimes to kill the sacrifice, when there was more work of that sort than the priest could conveniently perform (1 Chron. xxxiii. 28, 29; 2 Chron. xxix. 34, and chap. xxxv. 10—14). So that it was not necessary that the sacrifice should be slain by the Priest, as some erroneously suppose, alleging against the consideration of Christ's death as a proper sacrifice, that he must, in that case, in the character of a Priest, have slain himself." Bishop Clayton on the Hebrew Bible (p. 341), associates, according to Deut. xxxiii. 10, Priests and Levites in the service of teaching Jacob the Judgments, and Israel the Law, as well as putting incense and whole burnt-sacrifices on the altar. Bishop Colenso on the contrary, quotes Num. iii. 10, to show that the Priests must do the special work referred to, and that "the stranger that cometh nigh shall be put to death." But he does not also quote v. 9, which shows that the Levite is no "stranger." " And thou shalt give the Levites unto Aaron, and to his sons; they are wholly given unto him out of the children of Israel" (Read 1 Chron. xxiii. 24—32).

Here now I may allude to the distinction between the duties peculiar to the priests, and those in which the Levites might take part with them. The Levites were taken as the Lord's (Num. iii. 12, 41; viii. 14; xviii. 6). They are taken that they may minister to the Lord in holy things, and be to Aaron and his sons (Num. i. 50, 51; iii. 7, 9, 10; viii. 19, 24, 26). Now as to the peculiar duties of the priests, and those wherein the Levites might assist, we have a rather full account in Lev. xviii. 1—7. Therein we learn, that Aaron and his sons were to bear the iniquity of the sanctuary; they only were to minister before the tabernacle of witness; the peculiar inspection of the vessels of the sanctuary and the altar belonged to them; they only were to keep the charge of the sanctuary and of the altar. Particularly, it is evident from this, that Aaron and his sons alone might minister within the sanctuary; that the act of sprinkling the altar with blood especially belonged to them; and I need not add, that the sprinkling of the ark of testimony was the privileged duty of the high priest; and to the priests it was also assigned, to order all the sacrifices at the altar of burnt-offering. In all other duties, and in things contributing to the above-specified, the Levites might bear a part. By comparing Num. iii. 31, with xviii. 3, we might think there was discrepancy, but Num. iv. 15, 19, 20 will explain it all. The Levites might not go in of themselves, and look upon the sacred vessels; they must do after the appointment of the priests. In every other thing, they were to be full assistants to the priests.

Thus the one instance which the Bishop specifies, that of the offering after purification, might all be accomplished, even to the great extent which he calculates.

It is remarkable that all these offerings required to be offered at the Tabernacle, or afterwards at the Temple. The offerings at the Tabernacle were frequent, but as to the individuals they were rare. In the case mentioned above, the requirement to appear at the Tabernacle, or to go up to Jerusalem to the Tabernacle or the Temple, was only at the birth of each child. Many went up, though the goings up were not frequent to each individual, and the frequent journeyings of many served an important end. The frequent journeyings of the Israelites to Jerusalem served to promote the fellowship of brethren, and had this important effect, that the outward enactment and fulfilment, under penalty, kept them awake to the awful authority of Jehovah's law. In this book of the Bishop, the great intents of the Law are lost sight of, amid the eager desire to force a literal and limited interpretation upon the sacred history of Jehovah's ancient people.

To the unworthy digressions which occur in this chapter, I shall only briefly advert. The " turtle-doves or young pigeons " —Unbelief asks, Where were they to be found in such a desert? and Belief replies, The Lord knew, who had appointed them in sacrifice. Bishop Colenso cannot say, they were not found, though he deals so largely on the " waste howling wilderness." In one case, at least, provision is even made for one not able to make a offering of two turtle-doves or two young pigeons (Lev. v. 11. Canaan was not destitute of these birds, and we are not warranted in concluding, that they could not be found at all in neighbouring regions.

The large perquisites of the priests—How could they be consumed by so few? In the Lord's goodness, which this man cannot see, rich provision was hereby ordained for the priesthood of coming ages, when it would amount to a great number (1 Chron. xxiv.); and the mode of consumption at the beginning of the dispensation is indicated Ex. xii. 10; xvi. 19; Lev. vii. 17—19; viii. 32. The chiding by Moses, (Lev. x. 16) refers to their not having eaten at all, which Aaron accounts for, and Moses is satisfied. In ordinary cases, that which remained of their portion, when they had eaten in the holy place (Lev. vi. 25, 26) was to be consumed in fire.

The thirteen cities with so few to inherit them (Joshua xxi. 19). The suburbs were pretty extensive, but, as for what are called cities, these may have been small enough, for all which might be found representatives of Aaron. And it should be borne in mind that the Lord was providing as well for the future, when the family of Aaron should be increased to a multitude.

XVIII.—THE PRIESTS AT THE PASSOVER.

THE duties attending the second celebration of the Passover (Num. ix. 5) are the subject of Chap. xxi. of the Bishop's Book. Herein he treads on ground which he feels far from secure. Two impossibilities however, he attempts to show—the "sprinkling," and the place where, he says, the lambs must have been killed. This was the Court of the Tabernacle.

He states the two difficulties. It was the sprinkling of the blood of 150,000 lambs by three priests, in the space of two hours.

The other difficulty is this—All these lambs required to be killed in the Court of the Tabernacle, "before the Lord," at the door of the Tabernacle of the Congregation. In the small compass of the Court, 150,000 offerers had to appear with their offerings in the short space of two hours, thousands at one time.

The Bishop's proofs must be assigned, that we are to understand that the lambs were killed in the court, and that the blood was sprinkled on the altar by the priests. He refers to "the time of Hezekiath and Josiah when it was desired to keep the Passover strictly, in such sort as it was written, 2 Chron. xxx. 5;" whence he says, "the lambs were manifestly killed in the Court of the Temple," as the Paschal lambs in the wilderness were killed in the Court of the Tabernacle, whither all such offerings were brought, the blood being also sprinkled on the altar. He refers to the burnt-offering and the peace-offering for the manner of offering (Lev. i. iii.), and to the penalty of disobedience (Lev. xviii. 2-6). He also asks, by way of proving what he aims to establish, "How, in fact, could the Priests have sprinkled the blood at all, if this were not the case, that the animals were killed in the Court of the Tabernacle?" These are his proofs.

I regret to find that Kurtz, an able and judicious commentator, wanders much in his endeavours to meet such difficulties as hence arise. We must insist, THAT THE MINUTE DIRECTIONS CONTAINED IN THE INSTITUTION OF SACRIFICES MATERIALLY AND PRE-EMINENTLY INVOLVE THE FUTURE, when the system should have assumed in all respects, a sufficient degree of complement and completion; but, at once we acknowledge, *here* is an instance which we must meet, as it refers to the wilderness.

Did the priest sprinkle the blood of the paschal lambs at all in this second Passover which was held at Sinai? Were the lambs killed in the Court of the Tabernacle at all? No doubt in the time of Hezekiah and Josiah, the lambs of the Passover were killed at or near the Temple, probably in the Court (2 Chron. xxxv. 5), which was of large dimensions, and the blood was sprinkled by the priests upon the altar; but, as to the celebration of the Passover at Sinai, Dr. Colenso has still to prove that the directions he adduces for the burnt-offering and the peace-offering applied to the Passover in the wilderness. He may ask, Was the manner changed? Certainly it was changed —the manner of the first celebration of it, and that recorded in 2 Chronicles; and changed too under inspired men. When he has proved that the change took place at the second celebration, then we may be prepared to imagine ways and means whereby the animals might be killed near the Tabernacle, and the blood be sprinkled by the priests. Between the people and the priests, the medium of conveyance might well be filled up by the Levites, who might convey to the officiating priests the blood of many victims at once, so as to overtake the whole in the way of necessity. But the Bishop is a literal man, unrelenting in his demands, and he will admit of only one victim at a time. I, therefore, return to the question. Were the lambs killed in the court at all? Did the priests sprinkle the blood at all, in this second celebration of the Passover? The reference to the burnt-offering and the peace-offering avails not for the Paschal lamb, which was distinct; and his inquiry, How could the priests sprinkle unless the victims were killed in the court? shows how unsettled is the ground on which he advances. His reference to 2 Chron. xxx. 5, is much more to his point, which I shall now consider.

On this he builds his argument. The Passover had not been kept for a long time as it was written; consequently, it was kept right now, at this time of Hezekiah (2 Chron. xxx.), and afterwards in the time of Josiah (2 Chron. xxxv.). Hereby we learn that the people should have killed the lambs, but that, not being prepared, the Levites had the charge of the killing of the Passover for every one that was not clean, and flayed them (see also 2 Chron. xxix. 34); and the priests, receiving the blood from the hands of the Levites, sprinkled it. Bishop Colenso leaves it to be inferred that, with these specified exceptions, this was the manner in which the keeping of the Passover had been prescribed. Originally it was prescribed in quite a different manner (Ex. xii.); each head of a family sprinkling the blood on the door-posts and lintel, and all the family eating the lamb in their houses. Here, in 2 Chron. xxx., xxxv., the manner is changed. Did the change commence at the celebration of the Passover at Sinai? The answer remains in obscurity. Not a word of the change occurs in the account, Num. ix., or anywhere in these first books else, unless we find it in Deut. xii. 5—7, where directions are given as to the future; the Bishop would cover it over with the account of other sacrifices, the burnt-offering and the peace-offering, which we cannot allow; and not until we come to these passages in 2 Chronicles, do we find anything specific about the celebration of it, so that we are brought to the conclusion, that it was changed by David, or some other of Jehovah's servants, by inspiration of the Spirit. The Passover was kept at Sinai, which was the second time, and, as we would gather from the account, kept the same as at the first (Num. ix. 1—5, 9—12); and during all the thirty-eight years of wandering, we do not read of its being kept again (see Josh. v. 6—11). And though reference is made to keepings of the Passover (2 Kings xxiii. 22) in times succeeding, I am acquainted with no distinct mention of it till we come to the reigns of Hezekiah and Josiah. Till proof be adduced, therefore, that changes took place in the original mode of celebrating the Passover, we must hold that it was not changed in the wilderness; and we cannot speak definitively of change, till now that we are authorised by what we read in these later times. And what causes the Bishop to make so much of the expression, "in such sort as it was written?" (ver. 5). The sense conveyed seems to be, "for, in reference to the multitude, they had not done it as written, which is, All the people had not kept it." Our Translators may have founded upon ver. 18, which refers to the manner.

The Passover being kept at Sinai, then, as far as we know, much according to the original institution, with such variations as suited the circumstances, of which we know nothing, the *people* might slay their lamb, and sprinkle the blood, as a token that they confided themselves to the protecting care of Jehovah.

XIX.—THE WAR ON MIDIAN.

THE last chapter of objections to the Bible History in this strange book, is entitled "The War on Midian." We open it, expecting to find objections arrayed in the garb of argument; but, instead of this, there appear remarks addressed to the Laity of the Church of England, then a return to the numbers and events recorded concerning the Exodus; whence the Bishop brings together, culled from subsequent books of the Bible History, similar examples of exaggeration, showing, as he thinks, that the same disposition to magnify runs through all the Hebrew writers. This is the subject which he has long been contemplating with uneasiness; at first at a distance—then near.

Hereupon he expresses his thankfulness that "we are no longer obliged to believe as a matter of fact, of vital consequence to our eternal hope, the story related in Num. xxxi.;" and then he gives us the horrible recital. Having finished, he gives us in detail events which are said to have taken place at, and subsequent to this time, all within the last year of the wandering, and this that he may prove the utter impossibility of the thing. The Laity of the Church of England are able to defend their cause themselves, if they do not require that the Bishop himself be put into the position of defence. Numbers seem to have taken such hold of his mind that he must even dream of them. The most horrible images will haunt his midnight speculations. When the Bishop has shown that the numbers named in the historical part of Scripture, in relating the wars of Israel, are not borne out by the amount of population at the time, and the usages of war, an answer may be prepared. The Bishop having shown what he thinks the extravagant account given in the Scripture History, subjoins—" it being remembered that, at the battle of Waterloo, there were killed of the Allies . . . . . . only 4,172 men," quoting from Alison.

Alison writes thus :* " The total loss of Wellington's army, from the 15th to the 19th, was 20,290, including that of the Belgian and German auxiliaries, but exclusive of the Prussians, who lost 7000 more at Waterloo alone. The magnitude of the chasms in his ranks on this occasion, excited the most mournful feelings in the breast of the English general, and obliterated for a time all exultation at his triumph. The Prussian loss on the 16th and 18th, including the action at Wavre on the latter of these days, was 33,120. Of the French army, it is sufficient to say, that it was weakened on the field by at least 40,000 at Waterloo alone; but, in effect, it was totally destroyed; and scarcely any of the men who fought there ever again appeared in arms." (Alison's History of Europe, chap. xciv).

Here I have felt a strong temptation to run up through modern and ancient history, till we reach as near the times of Scripture History as history carries us, to convince the Bishop, if that were possible, that extraordinary numbers have been

* Killed, 4,172; wounded, 14,216; missing, 4,093; Total, 22,378 (22,481).

frequent in battle. But at present there is no occasion to enter the field of this heterogeneous chapter. As to the number stated in the Bible History respecting the Exodus, if such was the number, the Hebrew historian must record it.

The manner in which he speaks concerning the account of the war on Midian, is anything but becoming a prelate of the Church of England. At once in the spirit of raillery and abhorrence, as if first it were ridiculous to imagine that 12,000 Israelites were able to do it, and, next, that the deed were barbarous, gives expression to his warring thoughts. Taking him in the serious vein, we might say, he is here arraigning the righteous procedure of Jehovah. Of all the nations which had assailed Israel, the Midianites alone had treacherously attempted to draw them into idolatry. Allowed, their women had come forth with all their blandishments, seducing the men of Israel to open sin, and women were doomed to suffer. Nay, we admit, so far as concerned the present state of punishments and rewards, the awful retribution that had fallen upon the innocent. Certainly the young of the male population were cut off from the power of avenging their cause on the Israelites; and the young of the female population of Midian were amalgamated into the nation of Israel—thirty-two of them being specially devoted to Jehovah's peculiar service. Such was the terrible example. As Scott observes, had the destruction of the Midianites come by pestilence, famine, or earthquake, it would have been equally the Lord's doing. The record which is here, by no means carries us beyond what we frequently read of in history of the Lord's doings, if we believe in his over-ruling providence, in causing terrible desolations in the earth. The facts stand, but men have learned to look at them otherwise. Let us look at them aright; and not dare to arraign the righteous judgments of God.

One fling the Bishop will have at slavery before he dismiss this subject—"Jehovah's tribute of slaves' thirty-two persons." As a learned man, he will remember that slavery prevailed over the east from the earliest times. Now, here he cannot see, that the spirit of the Hebrew polity served to regulate the practice, and to introduce the better system that would uproot it. In this spirit, the female portion, taken in captivity, was devoted to the interest of the nation under law, and thirty-two of these were peculiarly appointed to the Lord's service as to the sanctuary.

But the Bishop will judge of Bible statements by their intrinsic value. In our simplicity, we should think, that if the writings, as a whole, were shown to be authentic, and evidenced accordingly by miracle, and the fulfilment of prophecy, to be divine; more especially were they attested (the writings of the Old Testament), by the highest authority to be the THE SCRIPTURES; and, moreover, did they unfold the very remedy that man needs for his poor stricken soul, we had enough. But this unbelieving Bishop will have nothing upon faith; he will try every single statement, of what value it is. By what will he try it? Human Reason. What is this human reason? The soul's apperception of things. But he must take this native power, as he finds it; it may all from first to last be a misconception. There may exist no such thing as consciousness, and an external world at all; Bishop Colenso may come to think himself one of Plato's pre-existent phantasms, let loose upon Natal in the shape of an English Bishop. Before he close this chapter he will show, by detailing a number of events that are said to have happened within a certain compass, how impossible it was that they could have happened. Observing that several of these events were *contemporaneous*, we can suppose that they might all happen in the course of the time, leaving the amount to each as indefinite as we find it.

But the Bishop is to leave no stone unturned, to have this whole matter settled to the satisfaction of Christendom. He has before him the work of settling the *age* or *ages* of these books of the Pentateuch, and the *manner* in which they have been composed. I do verily believe he may save himself the trouble. Much light may still be thrown on the field of sacred hermeneutics; but after the specimens Bishop Colenso has given, we shall hope from another quarter. He deals largely in the anticipatory; he has a golden vision before him—this Alnaschar in prelatic robes. Reverence dwells upon his lips, but in his designs, as judged by his writings, there is the rebellion of infidelity. He promises great consolation in his Commentary on the Romans, which I have not seen; but as a meet conclusion to such a work as this, he makes a woful reference to the faiths of the heathen, as if they contained the very essence of the Spirit of God speaking in man. Scarcely does the man need a Revelation from heaven who has these sublime mysteries, which he calls living truths. Late in the day, the Bishop has learned to adopt the later belief of the ancient world, that all the different religions were the worship of one God under different names—"Creator, Jove, or Lord." And having thus discovered, in the far south, the spring of light, the Bishop will discern all things and judge all things.

NOTES ON PART I.

In my Introduction, I have said, that Bishop Colenso takes not up what used to be considered the grand difficulties of the Bible History. In his Preface and Introduction, he talks on manifold subjects, of personal interest to himself, and, as he thinks, to the Church at large. Among the subjects of public interest, he alludes to Creation, but only alludes to it. In brief space he gives his opinion on the Deluge, without assigning his reasons; he goes not into the subject *in form*. This subject, which he more than once notices, I have remarked upon, and may do so again.

I observe that Dr. Cumming of London, intimating a course of Essays on Colenso's work on the Pentateuch, names the Deluge as one subject. Certainly, Colenso in his Preface does mention the Flood as one of the stumbling-blocks in the way of belief among his native Zulu. But he only mentions it together with his objection to the record, without going formally into the subject. Indeed, he only commences his formal objections when he takes up the subject of the Family of Judah. This is his first chapter of objections in form. Dr. Cumming, however, decides to take up the subject of the Flood. I know not if this be on the principle that every particle of a Bishop is precious—some may have a strong predilection to dignities; or rather, whether it may not be on the principle that there are some subjects which we like better than others. Dr. Cumming may also with ability take up the Bishop's real difficulties. As to the matter of the Flood, commentators have agreed to differ, without calling the good faith of one another in question, or questioning the authority of the historical of the Bible. Different from these, Colenso states broadly his dissent from the Bible account, which he authoritatively declares to be, that the Flood was universal as to the Earth. When Dr. Colenso states his objections in form, giving us the exegetics of the Old Testament account, exhibiting the universality of the Flood, and his reasons for disowning it, he will no doubt find those that will be prepared, both from his premises and his reasons, to meet him to the fullest extent, either on the side of a universal or of a partial flood, without impeachment either way of the divine record. Till this be done, it were too much to put arguments into Colenso's mouth, and then to take the trouble of refuting them.

An article in the *North British Review*, February, 1863, deals with the Bishop mildly. It expresses some surprise at his limited reading, and recent change of mind as to the credibility of the Bible history. It takes notice of the Bishop's rule of letting Reason decide on Bible statements what is worthy of God. Very justly is it observed, that we are not to measure ancient customs and modes of style by our modern ideas, especially if our ideas are of a limited kind.

This writer, entering into some of the details, takes up the Scripture account of Judah's family. On this subject he advances nothing new. Inadvertently he observes, that on perceiving the impossibility and even absurdity to which his conclusions led, Dr. Colenso should have abandoned them. Why, this is the very ground on which he proceeds to declare, that the account given is untrue. It was of no use that this writer should advert to the genealogy of our Lord as exhibited in the Gospels, to show that we must make allowances owing to our ignorance, for Dr. Colenso will equally pronounce these incredible. If the writer means to make out an argument, by referring to the mystical numbers, 7 and 10, and their product 70, equal to the number of Israel that went down to Egypt, he will find himself much mistaken as to Bishop Colenso. He is much more happy when he commingles this notion with the acknowledged fact of the "heads" of Israel, which he calls tribal stems.

I observe that the writer has imperfectly studied Colenso, making one of the difficulties in keeping the Passover in Egypt to be—Where pasture was to be got for grazing such a multitude of sheep as must have been according to the history. This difficulty the Bishop states only when the children of Israel are on their march and in the wilderness. The writer also tries to show how they might obtain as many lambs as would be required for the passover, a subject which Colenso does not here take up. The article, then, launches into the means of supply that might be in the wilderness, which is good enough; but then he makes up for any want that might be, by referring to the overruling providence of God, which he should know Colenso does not admit in this connection, there being no special mention of it.

Properly enough, the writer of this article, adverting to the genealogies, takes notice, that these genealogies, instead of exhausting the names of the families, give only the names of the heads of families. This is preparatory to entering upon the numbers. The writer is uncertain whether the 430 or 215 years should be adopted. I see, however, that on allowing the Bishop's calculation on the 215, this writer adopts the supposition, that many went down to Egypt with Jacob besides his children, and that by intermarrying with the Egyptians, and incorporation of them into Israel, the number of Jehovah's people was largely increased.

On the subject of numbers generally, and particularly on the number of the first-born, the writer acknowledges his incompetency to deal with the subject. He "indicates no definite opinion" respecting the numbers; and as to the results which Colenso brings out from the statement respecting the first-born, he simply says, "this is incredible." He gives in a foot-note, without endorsing it, an explanation, by the Rev. Dr. Forbes of Edinburgh, of the numbers, to the effect that a change in the notation has sometimes crept into the Hebrew Codices, equivalent to what the addition of a cipher would be in a modern account. Reducing the gross numbers by striking off a cipher, or by dividing by ten, the proportion of first-born would be 1 to 4·2 in a family, and the number of men 60,000. The writer of the article justly makes an exception to this mode of settling the difficulty, because it does not hold good in the first-born where there is no cipher in the figures marking the number. By striking off the cipher or the unite, and taking the difference between the first-born and the Levites as to number, the truth does not come out at all (Num. iii. 4—6). We might also add, the Hebrew numeration, in its mode of marking, does not rise or fall by tens, but by thousands. The Hebrews have single letters, counting from 1 up to 900; and then for the thousands they mark the single letters. Also by position of the letters, they designate numbers. The writer of the article subjoins, that "the numbers of the several tribes occur so frequently, and with so much circumstantiality, that we doubt extremely if any satisfactory solution can come from an alteration of these."

The writer adverts to the difficulty of exhibiting an account of early transactions in such a way as to be free from exceptions. Then the brevity and abruptness of the narrative will render the difficulty of comprehending all the greater. But he puts a case: Suppose the number of men to be limited to Colenso's mind, say 600, so limited a company might be easily conducted through the wilderness, but how should the puny host achieve for itself conquests so difficult, and grow in a few generations to a place and influence so mighty?

There follow remarks referring to the corroborations to the authenticity of the Bible history, which have been exhumed in Egypt and exposed at Nineveh. But more pointedly does he refer to the internal evidence of the divine books themselves—especially their high spirituality. Then, referring to the attestations which have been given to the authorship, he states what they, of Colenso's school, call the higher criticism, of allowing human reason to judge as to what is to be received as divine ; whereas he has shown that in presence of divine revelation, all flesh must be degraded. So far the Review.

The subject of slavery the Bishop mentions as one which, when apparently receiving countenance in the Hebrew Polity, excited the wonder and revulsion of the natives as might be expected. But the greater wonder is, that a Bishop of England was so little inclined to explain the policy of that Economy in the case—that the Hebrew Polity indeed began that system of amelioration whereby the superstition, and slavery, and sin that sprang up in the ancient world, were to be repressed, until those Gospel times should arrive, wherein full provision would appear for the complete emancipation of man.

I have adverted to the province which the Bishop would assign to Reason, in the matter of judging of the divine Word. In judging of Bible evidence, Reason will occupy a high position. The credibility of the books reputed divine will have to be tested, and the authority ascertained, by evidence. We are still gathering of this kind of evidence, in the fulfilment of prophecies which are taking place, and in viewing the corroborations to scripture history which are from time to time developed by trust-worthy travellers. We thereby go up to ancient times and customs as far as may be, without judging all by our modern ideas. Concerning the integrity of the books we have also to judge ; and means are ours by which to correct any mistranscriptions, and arrive at satisfactory assurance. On all these, and other acknowledged evidences, Reason will pronounce ; but when she has done so, Faith steps in and takes her high place. I need hardly say, that the Bible carries along with it its own evidence of its divine authority, in speaking with effect to the human heart, or rather, in being made to speak. The books of the Bible are before us, as a whole, so attested by highest authority, and ours it is to submit to the statements therein. Our best skill may be used that we may read aright what the books contain ; and having, according to the laws of language and thought, arrived at that, we are to receive with honest conviction. If we place Reason to tell us what we are to receive, and what not, there is an end of Revelation and of Faith. Hang up your Tablets around, say some contain the truth, others not, and bid us make the selection. They become all one with the writings of Zoroaster and Confucius. Take away the Pentateuch, take away the typical Ritual, take away the antitype, take away SALVATION. But the great essentials have stood unaffected, and standing, will reduce all the apparent anomalies to order and beauty. This literal Bishop will ruin his mind by his literality. It is observed by an able writer (Isaac Taylor), that he wants breadth of mind to judge of Old Testament narratives with necessary liberality. He does not allow that largeness to the Hebrew that he uses in his own English. He writes with the ease and plausibility of Hume; he insinuates, and leaves the insinuations to operate (see art. 46, 91, 129, 158). He insists on the literal ; he has no taste for measuring by the grand design. As to the literal exegesis, however, he should know that no code of grammatical rules can be formed that shall be without exception. Would he judge of even the flights of Homer, and the marvels of Herodotus, with the same unrelenting severity that he applies to the criticism of nature and simplicity, speaking in the Old Testament History ?

It were well did we remember, that we are out of our depth in calculating scripture statement. The doctrines are beyond our investigation : they were not discovered till revealed. The world by wisdom knew not God. If tradition told somewhat, it was borrowed. And the *historical* of scripture is beyond our times ; we should have lived at the times ; and even then, much would have had to be taken on faith.

Again I might ask, what motive the author of the Pentateuch had in making the statements we find? Was it all to magnify? Certainly the minuteness of discription lays him open to inspection. But if we look at the openness that every where appears, we shall be convinced it proceeds from divine inspiration.

The Bishop says it was the Zulu that quickened his suspicions. Rather we should think, the Bishop was inclined.

He has still a world before him. He speaks of advancing, in Part II., to the subject of the *dates* and *manner* of composition of these old records. He is to enter on the internal evidence, the styles of the different periods, and herein he will have the work of a lifetime.

But let him purify his mind of these suspicions, and come with the "honest" heart to the reading of the word. "Unto the upright there ariseth light in the darkness."

STRICTURES ON PART II.

On opening at the contents of Part II., we are struck with an array of nearly three pages of Corrections and Additions to be made in Part I., first edition. And, for the most part, these are not slips of the *type*, but of the *pen*. Scarcely can we bring our minds to think it justifiable, that a man should modify statements in a book subjected to much animadversion, by recommending the insertion of material *corrigenda et addenda*. I have already taken notice of the emendation he would make in chapter vi., concerning the priest having to carry the bullock out of the camp himself, and of the extraordinary admission he makes, that he might do this with the help of others. Writing, however, on the same subject (art. xvi.), I expressed my suspicion that Bishop Colenso saw through the strict meaning of the passage in Deut. xxiii. 12—14, that it referred to the army of Israel in Camp, and not to the whole body of Israel in the wilderness. I now see from these corrections and additions, that the Bishop was fully aware of this special reference to the army in Camp, for he now raises, as he thinks, an argument for himself out of it. He inquires, in effect, if the cautions laid down for an army were so necessary, how much more so would the same cautions be necessary for a mighty mass of people living in close proximity. This is plausible, but deceptious. We cannot allow the divine order to be applied save to that in reference to which it was prescribed, namely the army in Camp. But the Bishop asks, Was not cleanliness equally necessary for the people of Israel in the wilderness? It was equally necessary; but it was not prescribed to be attained by means of this special injunction, which had reference to the army.

I see also from these emendations, that the Bishop would be inclined to return to the subject of the Israelites being *armed* when they left Egypt. It may be remembered, that he inquired how they obtained the armour, how they had been let go with it, and how, when armed, they were afraid of a pursuing foe, being in such formidable number. He quotes to show that the Israelites had "swords," and "weapons of war," within the first and second year of their entrance on the wilderness. As before, so now we admit, they may by this time, or even at setting out, have had sundry kinds of weapons; but this improves not the Bishop's argument at all, that they are described as being "armed" when they left Egypt, for the original word still remains in its native dubiety, as we said. We have not to speak of them as if they were destitute of all things at their leaving

Egypt, and of all ingenuity after they had left; we have said the very contrary (Art. viii.), and here, like the Bishop, I might add, that by the end of the first year, they had waggons drawn by oxen (Num. vii. 1—3), given for the service of the sanctuary (v. 4—6); but we have to insist on this literal bishop, that he go not beyond the particular text on which he is building an argument. The children of Israel went up in array out of the land of Egypt (Ex. iii. 18).

In replying to his Reviewers, I observe that Bishop Colenso seems to depart from the spirit of candour, which he well maintained through Part I. At page xiii. of the Preface, he complains that they do not take up the real point of his argument as to the people assembling *at the door of the congregation*. The point of his argument, he says, distinctly was, that it is expressly stated in Lev. viii. 1, that Jehovah Himself summoned the congregation together, and that it is impossible to believe that Almighty God did really issue a command, which was not meant to be strictly obeyed—by all, at least, who were able to attend the summons. Well, let it be a divine command which all were bound to obey. The objection has been fully met—all attended there that were able, and the Bishop yet makes nothing more of it himself. He says, It was meant to be strictly obeyed—by all, at least, *who were able to attend the summons.*

In dealing with the Reviewers on the subject of the priest carrying forth the remains of the bullock without the camp, he is much consoled that one able writer holds the version which he has adopted to be the right one (Preface xiii.) Yet with all this countenance, the Bishop is "quite ready to admit that the Hebrew word here employed *may* be used in the sense of carrying out with the help of others." He adds, " But the stress of my argument is not laid upon the necessity of the priest himself in person doing this, but upon the fact, that it had *to be done by somebody.*" It is enough to say, Let any one read in the Bishop's sixth chapter how he uses the words—*to be carried by the priest himself—the priest having himself to carry*, and then say, whether the Bishop *bonâ fide* meant the priest himself. He will become a follower of Loyola in good time, and the name will be Spanish enough.

He notices also (Preface xiv.) the attempt of his Reviewers to meet the difficulties of the wilderness, by carrying the appointments forward to Canaan; and the Bishop renews the argument, that the particular instance—the turtle-doves for the poor leper—was intended for the wilderness, inasmuch as the leper had to go outside the camp. His argument here is good enough did it not admit of an exception, which I have shown (art. xvii.); and besides this, the argument against him for the *future* has reference, not to one solitary instance like this, but the whole typical economy.

The author of those Publications which we are considering thinks himself entitled to deal with the INTERNAL of Scripture, to examine the statements, and to judge of what is right (pp. 170, 205, 370). I think it were rather proper to say, We are to assure ourselves of the integrity and credibility of those reputed to be the Canonical Books of Scripture by the acknowledged evidence, and thereupon to apply the well-ascertained principles of interpretation to the exposition of Bible narrative and doctrine. But Dr. Colenso will deal with the Bible as he would with any human composition, judging the statements by the laws of human thought on subjects within his reach, while all the time many of the subjects on which he is engaged are so far removed from human reach as to have necessitated a Divine Revelation. He is now to account for the *contradictions* and *exaggerations* which he thinks he has found in Genesis.

How is he to do this? He is now "to consider the signs which these books of the Pentateuch give, upon close inspection, of the *manner*, and of the *age* or *ages*, in which they have been composed;" or, as he says in Part II., " to investigate thoroughly the question which has been raised as to the real origin, age, and authorship of the different portions of the Pentateuch."

The principles on which he proceeds are simple. He founds upon the appearance in Genesis of the two names of God, Elohim and Jehovah (see his chap. ii., Part II.); also upon the presence of certain proper names, and specially names of places, in Genesis and the other books of the Pentateuch (see chaps. v. and vi.) He adduces arguments arising from other grounds; but the two mentioned above are the prevailing ones through Part II.

Take the latter of the two modes—How does he build upon the presence, in Genesis and the other books of the Pentateuch, of certain names of offices, places, and things? Thus, names of places are found in Genesis which the places did not receive till long after the date of the history recorded in Genesis, and which some of them did not receive till the times of the book of Joshua, and subsequently. The same remark applies to the names of offices and things. The following are among the instances cited—Gilgal, Dan, Prophet, Hebrew, Canaanite, Canaanite and Perizzite, Hebron. This kind of objection to the credibility of the inspired record does not appear startling when we reflect, that a historian, Moses, might employ all the proper names known in his own time in recording events that took place before the names were assigned; that a subsequent inspired historian might insert the proper name where he found only a description; and that, finally, an explanation might, by the same divine direction, be inserted in the body of the narrative where it seemed to be required by readers at a subsequent age. The Bishop may say, as to such conjectures, the divine record should have been perfect at once. The record when first produced might be exactly suited to the wants of the people; but this might not be the case at an after age. These remarks will give readers an idea of what they have to expect in the Bishop's second book, and show what will be required in the way of answer.

Take, next, the former of the two modes of argument, namely, the use of the names Elohim (God) and Jehovah (Lord) in the book of Genesis. This fact appears to have furnished a main ground of argument in the Bishop's second book on the Pentateuch.

These two names occur frequently in the book of Genesis.

First, the name Jehovah is found in the record of Genesis, in the face of what is said in Ex. vi. 2, 3, "And God (Elohim) spake unto Moses, and said unto him, I am the Lord (Jehovah). And I appeared unto Abraham, unto Isaac, and unto Jacob, by *the name of* God Almighty (El-Shaddai); but by my name JEHOVAH was I not known to them." Yet we find, not only that the name Jehovah is frequently employed in the history before this time, but that the patriarch Abraham gave this, the incommunicable NAME, to the place of Jehovah's gracious appearance (Gen. xxii. 14). Likewise, we read that the Lord called himself by this name to Jacob (Gen. xxviii. 13), who twice immediately repeats this name (v. 16, 21). The explanation of this apparent discrepancy suggested by Scott, that the words in Ex. vi. 3, are to be read as interrogatory—but was I not known to them by my name Jehovah?—is neither required by the construction, nor by the sense of the passage, nor by the past history. Another interpretation proposed by others is much more agreeable to the genius of Hebrew naming—that while the Lord was known to the patriarchs as God, God Almighty, the All-sufficient to dependent creatures, he was not known as Jehovah, the only Existent, Existence itself, and the Author of all things, the import of the knowing being, that He was not known to them *experimentally* as the only All-Sufficient One, as explained, Ex. iii. 14, "And God said unto Moses, I AM THAT I AM." Yet with the exceptions mentioned already, scarcely can we say that the patriarchs ventured upon this name of Jehovah, or at all events, that they used it in the high sense of its being afterwards explained. In that remarkable passage where Abraham intercedes with the Lord in behalf of the cities of the plain, while the historian uses the name Jehovah, the suppliant addresses the Lord by the title Adonai. And this suggests the explanation given above, that the historian, in relating past events, might employ all the names known in his own later day.

Further, Bishop Colenso thinks he proves, that interpolations have obtained in the book of Genesis, in respect of this name Jehovah, from the single fact, that the name Jehovah was not really in use till the days of Samuel the prophet. His reasons for so thinking are two. Names begin in the time of Samuel to be compounded with the name Jehovah, which practice increases to a greater degree in the time of writing the Chronicles (pp. 224, 236, 357, 358). He finds in the Pentateuch and book of Joshua only two names so compounded, viz., Joshua and Jochebed. And names so compounded he does not find in the book of Judges at all. Again, the earlier psalms of David, who learned of Samuel, have rarely the name Jehovah, but frequently Elohim (pp. 269, 358). On the other hand, names compounded with the name El or Elohim are frequent in the history from the earliest times. Bishop Colenso thinks, therefore, he has reason for saying there were two writers, the one that uses the name Elohim, and another that also uses the name Jehovah; and that the latter is much later in the history than the former (pp. 176, 177, 207, 356). I find that the Bishop is arriving by degrees at a solution of the authorship of these ancient writings somewhat satisfactory to himself, that some good man, Moses for instance, originated the noble work of writing such a history (p. 368), which was taken up and wrought into a narrative from Genesis to Joshua, by the one that uses the name Elohim (p. 358), and who assumes the name Jehovah for the first time, Ex. vi. 2, 3 (pp. 234, 257), and then that his work was revised by the one that uses the name Jehovah. It is possible that Samuel may have been the one that uses the name Elohim, and some one at the end of David's time or later—Jeremiah say—may be the one that uses the name Jehovah, who would be the Deuteronomist. The writings of Moses, he believes, would have been respected had they really been of divine inspiration (p. 207), but it is evident, he thinks, that the Elohistic writer made free with those early documents, whatever they were, and that, correspondingly, the Jehovistic writer makes free enough with the writings of his predecessor. He speaks of the one as "altering, enlarging, or curtailing" what the other had done (p. 177); and, again, of the one taking the freedom to "enlarge, amend, and illustrate" the work of the other (p. 356).

Now, it will be remembered that all this reasoning is founded on the supposed fact, that names, till late in the history, are not compounded with the name Jehovah. I shall examine this point in one instance in the following paragraph. The whole history is set forth in the Bishop's book as a history of human composition (see also p. 368); but let us here ask, How was the name Jehovah made known, in its infinite significance, save in the way recorded—darkly, Gen. xxii. 14, 16; xxviii. 13; more clearly, Ex. iii. 14; distinctly, Ex. vi. 2, 3? And we ask, How came all these interpolations to be introduced, while the sacred books were in the keeping of men jealous in this respect, in the days of Samuel, and still more in the days of Jeremiah? The nation was blind enough, but among the priesthood, save in one instance (2 Kings xxii. 8), which, at the same time, afforded a proof of the reverence in which the divine word was held, there were always some zealous toward the Lord.

One entire chapter (ix.), he occupies on the name Moriah, being concerned to show that it is not compounded with the name Jehovah, and that the place signified is not the one on which the Temple came to be built. His main argument for passages in Genesis containing the name Jehovah, being interpolations of later date is, that names before the time of Samuel were not compounded with the name Jehovah, and were this name Moriah to be found to be so compounded, he would be afraid of his argument. I think he might assert, as in other names, that this was inserted at a later date. But he is bent upon proving that this name Moriah is not made up of any part of the name Jehovah. He sets himself to work to combat the opinion of Hengstenberg, who holds that the name Moriah was first formed on the occasion, when the Lord appeared to Abraham withholding him from immolating his son Isaac (Gen. xxii.), and that it is compounded of the Hophal participle of the verb *raah*, to see, and *Yah*, Jehovah. Hengstenberg renders the name *the shown of Jehovah—the appearance of Jehovah;* Bishop Colenso would rather think it means *being made to see Jehovah.* And I think the Bishop has here the advantage of the great German Exegesist, who sometimes makes his learning give way to interesting conceptions. The Bishop, however, is unhappy in the quotation he makes to support his interpretations (Lev. xiii. 49), *and the priest shall be shown it—shall be made to see it.* The literal is, *it shall be shown as to the priest.* The *eth* seems to perplex him, which contains a common rule, that the passive retains one of the two cases which the active governs.

The Bishop appears to be right as to the signification of the name Moriah, on the supposition that it is made up out of the verb *raah* and the name *Jehovah,* but he denies altogether this supposition. He will allow of no name being compounded with the name Jehovah till a late period of the history—towards the time of the Chronicles. Hengstenberg gives good reason for his opinion, but Bishop Colenso will argue the matter grammatically. The dropping of the *aleph* and the *he* is too much, he thinks, to be admissible, though he should remember that gutturals and vowel-consonants especially are frequently interchanged or elided, particularly in compounded names. And I think the parallel explanation found in 2 Chron. iii. 1, "Then Solomon began to build the house of the Lord at Jerusalem in Mount Moriah where *the Lord* appeared unto David his father, in the place that David had prepared in the thrashing-floor of Ornan the Jebusite," fully bears out the interpretation of the name Moriah. Thus (Gen. xxii. 2) "And he said, Take now thy Son, thine only Son, whom thou lovest—even Isaac, and get thee into the land of Moriah" (of being made to see—of being shown Jehovah). So to this corresponds the name which Abraham bestowed upon the place, v. 14, " And Abraham called the name of the place Jehovah-jireh ; As it is said to this day, In the mount of the Lord it shall be seen ;" or if the pointing would admit, in the mount, the Lord will be seen. So, 2 Chron. iii. 1, "And Solomon began to build the house of the Lord at Jerusalem in Mount Moriah (in the mount of being shown Jehovah), where the Lord was shown unto David his father."

The Bishop is pertinacious to do away with the idea, that any name compounded of Jehovah, appears in Genesis, or till late in the history. Having devoted one chapter to the name Moriah, he will yet require to devote another to the name, Judah, to show that it is not compounded of a verb signifying *to praise,* and the name *Jehovah.* "And she conceived, and bare a son ; and she said, This time will I praise the Lord (hapagham odeh eth Yehovah) : therefore she called his name Judah (*Yehudah*) Gen. xxix 35."

www.ingramcontent.com/pod-product-compliance
Lightning Source LLC
Chambersburg PA
CBHW031608110426
42742CB00037B/1326